Sister Mary Elizabeth Gintling

A Life For God

Tony Whall

ISBN 978-1-62806-065-2

Library of Congress Control Number 2015946981

Published by Salt Water Media
29 Broad Street, Suite 104
Berlin, Maryland 21811
www.saltwatermedia.com

Cover photograph by Bob Sprengel. Printed with permisssion from Catholic Extension. Copyright © 2015 www.catholicextension.org. This photo appeared on the cover of Extension Magazine in October 1989.

Dedicated

to

The Little Sisters of Jesus and Mary

"Lord, who may dwell in your sanctuary?
Who may live on your holy hill?"

Table of Contents

Preface
&
Acknowledgements

I volunteered as an interviewer at the Joseph House Crisis Center in 1986 until I left to work with the local Habitat for Humanity chapter the following year. Because the two organizations often served the same clients, I maintained a close and, for Habitat, beneficial relationship with the Little Sisters of Jesus and Mary for many years after my brief tenure there. I would also cross paths with the sisters at church and in the neighborhood, our houses being but one block apart.

After Mass one morning in 2012, I told Sr. Connie, the Mother Superior of the Order since 2002, that I wanted to work with Joseph House again and I asked if there was anything she could think of for me to do. Without hesitation, she said, "Yes, you can write a book about Sr. Mary Elizabeth." It took me a few awkward seconds to realize that she was not kidding and that, despite my suspicion that I was not qualified to undertake such a project, she believed that I was (months into the work, I confessed to her again that I still wasn't certain I was the right person for the job. "You're all we've got," she replied, with blunt, puckish candor).

So I toiled away, reading everything I could by and about Sr. Mary Elizabeth, and interviewing many people who lived and worked and prayed with her, and gradually the portrait of this holy woman who lived for God revealed itself as it is found in these pages. And as I worked, I became increasingly grateful for having been summoned to this task. Each day I was more awed by this nun's passionate goodness, indomitable spirit and fervor for the poor. I felt blessed to be in her company, despite her having been dead ten years.

I was blessed, too, to spend many days over a year's span listening to the recollections of men and women who accepted the invitation extended by Sr. Mary Elizabeth to devote their lives to her mission, and who were willing to share those memories and estimations with me. Those hours were, for me, gently restorative, a recurring reminder of the unflagging goodness of so many people, many of whom continue the work begun by Sr. Mary Elizabeth almost fifty years ago.

It is to them that I dedicate this book and to

whom I acknowledge my profound debt and my thanks. I want especially to express my gratitude to Dan McDonald who made the archives of the Little Sisters of Jesus and Mary available to me, directed me to those materials that would most benefit this project and, most substantially, shared with me the transcriptions of many hours of interviews he had conducted with Sr. Mary Elizabeth from which, unless otherwise indicated, Sister's testimony in this book is drawn. Dan also proofread an early manuscript of the book, calling attention to errors of fact and language and questioning the emendations I have made to written and spoken documents for the sake of brevity, amplification and clarification. I wish to express to him my thanks for his corrections and suggestions.

Heartfelt thanks, too, to Anne Cuomo for her friendship, generosity, serene good spirits, and wise counsel.

Finally, I want this book to be a testimony of my love for my family–Carol, John, Kevin, and Alison. Loving them has made the yoke of my life easy and the burden light.

Introduction

Early in the evening of October 26th, 2004, Sr. Marilyn tidied up in Sr. Mary Elizabeth's bedroom in the Little Sisters of Jesus and Mary Novitiate in Princess Anne, Maryland, hoping to hasten Sr. Mary Elizabeth into bed after a busy day of meetings, of writing letters, of signing checks. Sr. Mary Elizabeth was recovering from an especially debilitating bout of pneumonia and Sr. Marilyn wanted her to continue her recovery by getting as much rest as she could. Sr. Mary Elizabeth was in her bathroom preparing for bed. She called to Sr. Marilyn and showed her what she had just spit up. There was no doubt in either of their minds that it was blood, dark and thick.

Earlier that day Sr. Mary Elizabeth had spit up pink fluid and Sr. Marilyn had called Dr. Joseph Badros in Salisbury, Sr. Mary Elizabeth's attending physician and one of her closest friends, who surmised that Sister's throat had been inflamed by the cough caused by the pneumonia. But as Sr. Mary Elizabeth continued to cough up more and more blood, Sr. Marilyn got alarmed, especially when she realized that Sister was also having trouble with her breathing. Sr. Marilyn had heard similar sounds often before; Sr. Mary Elizabeth, at 89, had suffered for many years from Chronic Obstructive Pulmonary Disease that had severely weakened her heart and left her fettered to an oxygen tank by a tubular tether she referred to as her trunk.

But what Sr. Marilyn saw now frightened her despite her realization for the past few years she served as Sr. Mary Elizabeth's assistant and constant companion that a day such as this would surely come. Sr. Mary Elizabeth was struggling to breathe. The front of her nightgown was spattered with blood, and the panic in her eyes and gestures conveyed unmistakably that she was choking on her own blood. Sr. Marilyn ran to the intercom to call the other sisters for help, and, in a barely audible voice, Sr. Mary Elizabeth gasped, "You'd better call 911!" before she lost consciousness.

Those who knew Sr. Mary Elizabeth would not have been surprised at her final instruction. "Get me to the hospital!" she was saying. "Get me repaired! I've got so much to do tomorrow!" She was famous for putting all her trust in God's will, of proclaiming perpetually that we must rely on God's wisdom and love to guide our every step. But when it came to her own dying, she and God seem to have been on different pages. She had done so much, but she had so much more to do, so much suffering to assuage, so many burdens to lighten. She simply could not die just yet, despite her age, her congestive heart failure, her lungs collapsing slowly and filling with blood, despite the strokes and falls and broken bones. "Call 911!"

Sr. Marilyn asked the other sisters to call 911, Dr. Badros, and the convent in Salisbury to notify Sr. Connie Ladd who had been elected Superior General of the order in 2002. As they called, Sr. Marilyn laid Sr. Mary Elizabeth on the floor on her side to help her breathing, and tried to clear her lungs of blood. As she worked, she whispered, "Don't die, Sister, please don't die."

The EMT's raced to Sr. Mary Elizabeth's aid. They knew the little nun, knew that she was known as the Mother Teresa of Salisbury by many and as Mother Goose by those who loved her and labored by her side. They had transported her many times from Princess Anne to Salisbury. "You should be getting frequent flyer miles," one of them joked on one of their recent trips. This time they knew immediately that her condition was grave. Sirens blaring, they sped along the darkening highway toward the hospital, trying to clear her lungs so she could breathe. Sr. Mary Elizabeth began to turn blue. And halfway to Salisbury the ambulance broke down.

The response team worked frantically to keep Sr. Mary Elizabeth alive while waiting for the backup ambulance. At the hospital, the apprehensions of the crowd that had gathered at the ER entrance, now grown to close to a dozen, mounted as the minutes dragged past. Where could they be? What had happened? Did they change their minds? Perhaps it was not as bad as Sr. Marilyn had at first surmised? Or, was it the worst? Were they taking their time because there was no need to rush, now that it was over? But to have her slip away without a chance to say goodbye, to tell her that they loved her, that was an intolerable finale none could imagine or bear.

The ambulance pulled up to the ER dock. The community wanted to accompany Sr. Mary Elizabeth but the medical team didn't want them to see her until the bloody gown was replaced and she was resting more quietly. So they waited some more, praying together, comforting each other.

In her room, they surrounded her bed. She was unconscious and festooned with tubes and lines and wires, a veritably insensible, blessed porcupine. Her devoted followers took turns whispering to her, touching her, comforting her however they could. One of them began to sing the anthem of their order, "The Servant Song," and soon all had joined in, singing softly so as not to disturb the other patients and their families in the Critical Care Unit. "Will you let me be your servant," they sang, "Let me be as Christ to you?" They were sure she could hear them and that she was singing along in her heart. "I will hold the Christ light for you, / In the night time of your fear; / I will hold my hand out to you, / Speak the peace you long to hear."

But their dear Mother Goose lay there, comatose, swollen and grey, far beyond their melody, far beyond fear, nearer to Christ's light than they could imagine. The duty nurse called Sr. Connie into the hall. Sr. Connie returned, grieving but resolute. Sister is being kept alive mechanically, she informed them. She cannot survive on her own. We must let her go to her Father. And so it was agreed to discontinue life support and let Sr. Mary Elizabeth die.

As the sun rose in the early morning hours of October 27th, 2004, Sr. Mary Elizabeth Gintling passed out of this world two months shy of her 90th birthday. Her body went into the ground, but her spirit keeps on to this day guiding and inspiring hundreds of followers who labor in the vineyard she planted and nurtured on the Eastern Shore of Maryland. This book is the story of the woman possessed of that extraordinary spirit, of her life and work, and of the remarkable ministry that remains as the bountiful legacy that was her enduring gift to the world.

In the Beginning

Mary Elizabeth Gintling was born in 1914, the third--and only girl--of Henry and Dessie Gintling's five children. Her family moved from Philadelphia to the Sparrows Point neighborhood of Baltimore shortly after Mary Elizabeth (or "Mae," as she was called) was born.

Her father had only a third grade education but was possessed of an inquiring mind and an adventurous spirit. He had quit school to work to support his family and, as a young boy, he gave tours of the Gettysburg battlefield, and searched for Civil War artifacts to sell to tourists and collectors. He seemed to have been born with the instincts of a pioneer, with a desire to do things no one else had done. He helped build the first electric plant in Littleton Pennsylvania; he drove trains around the famed Horseshoe Curve in Logan Township, Pennsylvania; when automobiles were the newest craze for those wealthy enough to afford them, he drove them from the factories in the Midwest to their new owners along the East Coast.

Mae adored her father. "I think his greatest claim to fame was that he lived from the age of the wagon wheel to the age of space flight, when a man walked on the moon," she said. She admired his intelligence and adventurousness and entrepreneurial spirit (three traits exhibited later in the endeavors of his devoted young daughter). "He supported his growing family as an automobile mechanic, but he supplemented his income by opening one of the first movie theaters in Baltimore. And he had this magic act that he'd perform in theaters around the city. He learned all these things reading books after having gotten only to the third grade. He even built the house we grew up in after studying books about construction, electricity and plumbing. He was a remarkable man." [Mae loved construction. Many years later, at the Salisbury convent, Mae, now Sr. Mary Elizabeth, almost 70 and burdened by the oxygen tank that had become her constant appendage, had to be persuaded to not roll up her sleeves and start shoveling concrete for the fish pond she wanted for the back yard of Brother Charles Place, a residence for visitors next to the convent.]

The Gintlings were poor, "but we never knew we were poor," Sister insisted. Poverty taught them all how to live frugally. "No matter how poor they were, my parents always saved something. My father would never buy anything on credit and he didn't allow my mother to buy anything on time. They either had the money or they went without." She and her brothers learned very quickly that they couldn't have many of the things their classmates took for granted. "We often walked to school to save the streetcar fare. We bought day-old bread from the local bakery. But we were really very happy children and I think living this way helped us to deal with the challenges of life later on. Poverty for us wasn't a burden; it was a challenge."

Mae was the recipient of well-worn "hand-me-down" clothes given to her by an older cousin, and often her schoolmates were less than charitable with their observations about her attire. "I somehow learned from my mother that nice clothes did not mean you were a nice person. So when someone snickered at my clothes, I knew they weren't snickering at me." It was difficult, though, being ridiculed, but Sister concluded she got a good moral foundation in life because she learned that it didn't matter what clothes one wore, or what work one's father did, or how much money one had. "I was the first female class president at Sparrows Point High School, and, believe me, I was the worst-dressed there, too," she recalled, laughing at her memories of those times. "My parents taught us what really matters in this life," she said quietly.

"My mother was very small, very nimble, *very* neat. She would instruct the girls who were intent on marrying her sons never to be in their aprons when their husbands returned from work. Don't have your hair in curlers; fix yourself up like you would for your boyfriend. She always looked lovely when my father came home, and she would have his slippers out for him and the newspaper on the table next to his chair. It was good to learn that kind of respect when we were children.

"I never heard my parents argue. Never. When

I first heard a man and woman arguing, I thought, well they're not married," she said, laughing at this recollection. "My father was the head of that household, but he was a very unthreatening person. He would say to us sometimes, 'If I ever whack you. . .' But we knew he would never hit us, and he never did."

"I remember being sick as a child, and after work he would bring me supper in my room, and after I had eaten, he would sit under the gas lamp in the hallway and read stories to me and to any of the others who were in bed by then. We would hear his voice, coming into the room from the hallway. He was a good daddy. He certainly was. He always provided well for us, did kind things for us. We knew we could always depend on him. No foolishness, but fun, real fun, yes."

Once her father split his finger on the flywheel of a car that someone accidentally turned on when he was working on it. "My poor mother was so upset; she ran crying to the house, not knowing what to do. I was about 14. My father held the finger together, blood dripping profusely from the wound. 'Can you help me with this?' he asked me. 'What can I do?' I asked him. 'Get me a clean rag from the house and cut it into strips.' I tied the strips around the finger to hold it together. When I had finished, he opened a can of varnish and stuck his finger into the varnish. I can still see the look of pain on his face, but he never uttered a sound. When he took the strips off many days later, the finger was healed perfectly. He did everything like that."

"My mother was a good, simple woman. We had a neighbor in Sparrows Point whose husband was dying. She came to my mother in tears and told her that she was frightened, and that she couldn't take care of him, and especially could not bear to be with him when he died. My mother told her to go home and take care of him and to make believe he was someone else, and when it came time for him to die, my mother would stay with him. I went with her at the appointed time, taking the blessed candles and holy water. These people weren't Catholics, but my mother said to the dying man, 'Now, Mr. Hermanof, I think God is going to take you to Heaven tonight so I am going to stay with you. I don't want you to be alone. I just want to tell you about God. He loves you very much. There's nothing to be afraid of; you will just wait until He says, "Come," and then you are going to go and He is going to be very good to you. He made you because He loves you, and He is calling you now because He loves you and wants you to be with Him in Heaven. I am going to light the blessed candles to keep all the devils away, and I have holy water here. There is nothing to worry about.' And that man died in perfect peace. It was all pretty simple to her!"

The Gintling children knew that their parents couldn't afford to spend any of their income on school. The family moved to Sparrows Point in Baltimore near the steel mill where her father and oldest brother, Harry, had gotten jobs. Roger, the second of the boys, also worked in the mill but went to school in the evenings and eventually got his law degree from the University of Maryland. Quickly discovering that he was not suited for the law, he went back to school—all the time working at the mill—and got a naval engineering degree at Johns Hopkins. He worked for the government as a naval architect. "He lived on a farm north of Baltimore, and if the winter weather made it impossible for him to drive into the city, they'd send a helicopter to pick him up. He was a very important person in that organization," Sister recalls proudly, "and, like my father, he did it all on his own."

At church one Sunday, three-year old Mae saw a nun. She asked her mother about that woman in the black nightgown. Her mother told her that the woman was a nun, that they were the wives of Jesus and spent their lives helping people for Jesus' sake. From that moment, Sr. Mary Elizabeth said, "I knew that is what I had to be. What attracted me so much is that they belonged to God, and I knew somehow that I belonged to God, too. I wasn't sure what that meant, but I knew that's what I wanted to be." Three years later, walking with her mother through a poor neighborhood near Sparrows Point, little Mae was upset by the squalor through which they walked. Her mother explained that the people here didn't have money to buy anything, sometimes even food, and that some of the families were too poor to let their children go to school. Worse, they might suffer so much that they didn't believe that God loved them. Sr. Mary Elizabeth would point to that experience as another in her journey to the religious life. "I vowed that night that I would dedicate my life to helping the poor," she recalled. "In my whole life I have never been interested in anything but doing things for God," she said, as if she were having this insight for the first time. "I can't not do what I do—it's almost as if I have no choice in the matter."

"When I was about 10 years old, I was reading The Lives of the Saints, and I decided to make a vow of chastity and devote myself entirely to God. So I asked my confessor if I could make a vow of chastity. Needless to say, he was just a little bit puzzled," she laughs. He said he'd have to ask the bishop. 'When will you see him?' I asked. 'Well, I don't see him every day,' he said. 'Well, when you see him, would you ask him?' And, to my surprise, he did, and I was allowed to take a vow of chastity, but not until I was 14 or 15."

Sr. Mary Elizabeth said her family wasn't overtly religious, but once she made her First Holy Communion, she remembered that she wanted to go to Communion every day for the rest of her life. "My father, who had a touch of the Jansenist in him, objected. He felt I wasn't holy enough to attend daily Mass. 'But I thought that's how you become holy,' I argued." She laughed, recalling this early religious debate. "I went to confession and the priest asked if my father had forbidden my attendance. When I said no, he assured me it was alright for me to celebrate the Eucharist every day, 'but if he ever tells you not to go, then you can't go.' He never forbade me; he simply thought I wasn't good enough to go!"

Mae attended Saint Ann's Parish School near

Mary Elizabeth ("Mae") Gintling, early 1930s

her home and at age 12, she presented herself to the teaching nuns in that school as a candidate for their convent. "I was devastated when they told me to wait five years," she said. Another crushing rejection came when, age 19 and a novice with the School Sisters of Notre Dame, "I was told my vocation lay elsewhere, and not as a teacher with their community. My whole world turned upside down." But she would admit later in her life that their rejection had been another instance of God guiding her to her true vocation. She was not, she acknowledged, an ideal candidate for the classroom. Her foremost desire was still, as it had been since childhood, to mitigate the suffering of the poor.

She decided that nursing was her calling, and in 1941 she graduated from Mercy Hospital's Nursing School in Baltimore and after working as a public health nurse for two years she entered the Little Sisters of the Poor, a community dedicated to caring for the elderly poor and the incapacitated nuns of the order.

"I was quite old [she was 29] when I became a nun. When I told my mother I wanted to join a convent, she said, 'Oh, child, think about this; they will try you very hard and you will have to clean out the cracks of the floor with a pin.' " Again, Sister laughs at this memory. She wonders where her mother had heard such stories. "So I said to her, 'Mother, you can only do one thing at one time in life. If you are cleaning out the cracks in the floor with a pin, you are not doing something else. It doesn't matter what you are doing, so long as you are doing it for God's sake, for the love of God.' "

She spent four years in France before taking her final vows. Life in France was difficult for many of the younger novices, but not for Mae Gintling who had grown up poor in the country near Baltimore. "We didn't have running water in our house for many years while I was growing up, so washing in cold water at the sink in France wasn't as much of a hardship for me as for the girls from more comfortable families. When we got our one annual bath at the mother house in Riems, sometimes a daddy long-legs would attempt to join you, and sometimes the old pipes ran with black silt, and it was hard to decide to get into that tub!"

In those days, Sister recalled, no one had any family come over for the celebration of their final vows. No family came, not even if they lived next door. "I like that idea—that this is an intensely private commitment of your life to God, and that there would be no outside distractions. One celebrated this moment with the women one served God with. It was nice; it certainly built a sense of community to have it that way." Sister thought for a moment, then added, "I do see my life as a sister as a marriage, very much so."

For the next 21 years, as Sr. Armel de la Providence, she tended to the physical and spiritual needs of the residents of nursing homes in several cities in the East and Midwest, in New York, Washington, Baltimore, Cleveland, Louisville and Detroit, among other places. In New York she was called upon to use her professional nurse's training for the first time. She was the only one with a nursing degree. None of the other sisters—who spent their lives nursing the poor and elderly—had any training at all. Increasingly there was pressure from public health officials to ensure that those caring for the elderly had professional training. Medically, the care had been mediocre, Sr. Mary Elizabeth acknowledged, but the sisters' devotion to those in their care excelled. "So they began training the sisters, adding knowledge to their devotion, and then you could have paid a billion dollars and not have gotten better care than the care provided by the Little Sisters of the Poor."

What really troubled Sr. Armel was the number of needy people turned away for lack of space and financial support. "Sometimes we would have a waiting list of 30 or 40 people, most of whom were in their 60's and 70's. It's one thing to be on a list like that when you're in your 20's, but it's terrible to be old and in need of help and protection and to be put on a waiting list that no one bothers with." The community did not approve of Sr. Armel's urgent recommendations about helping those on the lists.

"I began to realize after many years that I could not go along with their old-fashioned ways of doing things and the way they discouraged any ideas to improve things. I guess this was a manifestation of the culture they had inherited from France. So more and more I began to feel that I could do a lot more for people if I were able to get away from the restrictive regulations that bound the order. I devised plans that would allow me some independence but would allow me also to remain part of the community, but they wouldn't hear of it. Then I began to think that maybe God was calling me to leave. But, you know, I didn't want to go back into the world for anything. I was 45 years old when I started to undergo this struggle. I had been a Little Sister for fifteen years."

A Heavenly Call or a "Passport To Hell"

Sr. Armel was, she insists, very happy nursing the elderly, "but I knew God was calling me to go out to the poorest of the poor and to find them and love them in their own neighborhoods and homes." She went to her confessor more than once, explaining her desire which, she said, was as strong a call as that which brought her to profess her final vows. He wouldn't permit such a thing, she said. "He told me, 'I don't want to hear about it. I don't have time today to hear confessions. I just don't want to hear about it.' He told me to forget it and to get back to my real work. So, I thought, I guess God doesn't want to hear about it, either!" For five more years Sr. Armel obeyed his decree, but, as she recalls, she was so troubled by the yearning. "I felt pushed by some force to leave there and start something on my own.

"I had this impulse that I couldn't seem to overcome, and I got so tired of battling with it. So I said to God, 'Look, I'll do anything You want me to do, but I have to know that You want me to do it and I

**Sr. Armel de la Providence,
Little Sisters of the Poor, 1948**

want You to at least give me the assurance that this is something You want and not just something that I dreamed up for myself.' So I kind of put Him to the test."

Then, in 1964, she tried again. As she told Father Patrick Brankin for an interview in Extension magazine in 1987, "I knew that God couldn't ask me to do something and at the same time not give me the means to do it, so I decided again to see if God was serious.

"Before I spoke with my confessor, I knelt down at the Communion rail and prayed: 'Look, God, I'm going to ask Father again, and if he says "yes," then I'll do it. I won't look back and I won't count the cost. But if Father says "no," well, it's "no." Then for good measure, before I finished, I told God he had two and a half minutes to get Father ready.

"Father was a real old crusty sort. I went in and asked him if he remembered that five years before I had asked him if God could be calling me to do something more for the poor. He said, 'Of course I remember you, Sister. I am convinced that God wants you to serve Him this way.'

"Well, I was so shocked! My first thought was, 'It's not fair!' I told God, 'I'm 50 years old. Lord, I don't know the first thing about starting a religious congregation!'" But she knew then that God had spoken to and through her confessor, and that she was now obligated to leave the order she had faithfully served for over 20 years and embark on a new and utterly unchartered path. It was a daunting prospect, but Sr. Armel was buoyed by an unconditional faith in Divine Providence. If God wanted her to begin again, to undertake a new ministry serving the poor by living among them, she knew she would succeed. If she failed, she was certain, God would guide her to the right path.

"So many of these thoughts were flashing through my mind, until I heard Father say, 'You're not hearing what I'm saying!' I was floored. I said, 'Oh, were you talking to me?' " she laughs. 'Yes,' he said, 'I want you to understand how your Little Sisters are going to react to this. It isn't going to be easy. They will not want to let you go, and they will make it very difficult for you to leave. But I want you to know that you have my permission to do it because I really do believe you've been called to serve God in another way.' And I thought, a bit fearfully, well this is something different. And this was the beginning of my struggle to work my way through a very unpleasant event." [1]

It became obvious at once that Sr. Armel's confessor knew what he was talking about. It was, we will see, an understatement to say that leaving the Little Sisters in 1964 was a very painful experience. Her superiors did not want her to leave, and, though she knew she was following the path God was directing her to take, she felt the pull of the familiar life she had lived for 21 years and of the close friendships she had forged over those many years. She wrote to the Mother General of the order, asking if she could serve in another way while remaining a member of

---

1   Brankin, Fr. Patrick. "A New Community Grows." Extension August/September, 1987: 12-15

the community. Her superior took this letter with her when she went to spend a month at the head-quarters in Paris.

"I heard nothing all the time she was gone, and when she returned she said nothing to me about my request. One day I couldn't stand it any longer, so I got up the courage to ask Mother if she had given my letter to Mother General. She told me she certainly had. 'Did she give you an answer?' I asked. 'No, I think she is thinking about it, Sister,' she replied. 'So what do I do now?' I asked. 'Well, Sister, you just go on doing your work.' " Sr. Mary Elizabeth, recall-ing these days twenty-five years later, laughs softly at the memory of what must have been, at the time, a painful and frustrating encounter.

It did not get any easier. Sometime later her superior called Sr. Armel into her office and handed her an envelope. She told her she had had the letter from the Mother General for quite some time but was reluctant to show it to her. " 'The General has rejected your request and has made it clear that no special consideration will be given to you.' She told me that if I were going to leave, then I'd have to do it the way it had always been done. I'd have to write a letter asking that my vows be terminated, and that this request would have to go through the chancery office. What's more, I was to leave the house I had been living in for so many years and move into the novitiate house while waiting for an answer from the diocesan chancellor."

At her appointed time she was greeted by an old monsignor who ushered Sr. Armel into his office and rudely exclaimed, "Oh, good God, another one of these nuns who's going to tell me all the holy things she's going to do, so that she can get out of the convent!" Sister told him she wasn't going to tell him such things, only that she felt God was calling her to another path. "Oh, they all say the same thing! Do you realize that you are signing a paper that is going to send you straight to Hell?!" She told him she thought this was what God wanted. "Oh, and how are you so certain about what God wants?! Well, come on, get it over with. You sign this request, and when the approval comes from Rome, I will send for you."

Sr. Armel felt like a prisoner in the novice residence. "I was totally ostracized. I reported to the superior of novices. When she saw me, she said, 'Oh, you. I don't even want to talk to you. You go on upstairs; someone will assign you a room.' This superior was a youngster whom I had helped many times over the years. I went upstairs, and I thought that I would have to work very hard to not get discouraged. Now that I have made this decision, with God's guidance, I must put up with things without complaint." She was assigned a bed where she had to stay during the day. She was allowed to walk in the yard, but only in a section the novices didn't use. "So much time passed, and I never had any connection with the novices at all," she said. At recreation, she had to sit near the superior, but no one talked to her, so it made little difference where she sat.

But something wonderful happened to her

during this lonely time—"the time of my house arrest," she laughs. "I wanted to spend my time in a positive way, even though it was a rather negative experience. In the library I found a book, *The Mystical Body of Christ*. I wish I still had it, wish I could recall the author." Each day, walking in the garden, she would fall into profound meditative states based on her readings in this book, a penetrating examination of the meaning of the mystical body.

"One day, while walking in the garden under the influence of this meditation, I had what I suppose must be called an intuition into the depths of this mystery of the mystical body. I saw how Christ bridged all time and that not only had He been crucified at an historical point in time, but that He was still being crucified, that He had been born and was still being born. I comprehended with such utter clarity that Christ was being born and was suffering and dying, and that it was going on as if no time was passing at all. All time was in each moment. The insight was so evident that I couldn't understand how I had not seen it before.

"I could not grasp what was happening to me, but it was as if I weren't even walking on the ground. I seemed to be above the ground, to be out of the world. Gradually I began to feel the earth beneath my feet again. I longed to describe what had happened to me but I couldn't find the words. But I realized later that this experience was what sustained me during my entry back into the world."

Months passed, and she became aware with dread that December 8th was approaching, the day on which everyone renewed their vows. Sr. Armel wondered what she should do, what she could do. The congregation held a retreat preceding vow day, which gave her a chance to discuss her dilemma with a confessor. "I remember saying to him, quite seriously and with a good deal of anxiety, 'Father, tomorrow when we're supposed to renew our vows publicly, one by one, I am scared that everyone will be watching me wondering if God is going to strike me dead. What should I do? Should I even be there? As I'm sure you know, I've requested a dispensation from Rome.' He was very kind and understanding and he said, 'Sister, you think you are doing what God wants you to do. You still have your vows. Renew them.' So I did. I think it was one of the hardest things I've ever done." A few days later her dispensation arrived from the Vatican.

But this was months after she submitted her request. During that lonely, friendless time, she would attend reflection sessions which featured recordings of homilies, many of which mourned those who had lost their vocation and had left the convent. The sisters would sit quietly, and Sr. Armel was certain they were all looking at her, and, she said with a certain degree of understatement, "It was kind of rough."

The time dragged by, month after month, without hearing from Rome. She became convinced they were trying to break her resolve, and if they were, they were succeeding. She thought that perhaps she had made a mistake, and that God was giving her a chance to retract her petition. She decided to leave her fate in the hands of the community's Provincial; if Mother thought she was wrong, and would have her back, Sr. Armel would accede to this destiny. And now she tells of a perplexing and extraordinary occurrence: "I fetched a new writing pad I had purchased to record my reflections. I opened it. There, on the first page, was a poem in my handwriting, a poem about a new order I was starting, an order devoted to Mary. I was dumb-struck. Here is my handwriting, but I hadn't written this. I tore the page out and went to stick it into the back of the pad—and there was another poem, by my hand, describing the new community!"

"I felt I was going mad. I went into my room and picked up my Bible. I remember saying to God, 'I hate it when others do this, but I'm going to do it. I can't live like this. I need a sign, I need to know that this is what you want me to do.' So I opened the New Testament at random, and St. Paul was telling the Greeks, or Romans, maybe, that he would free them from the law and put a new heart in them. I don't remember where he said this, but I remember the part about rescue from the bonds of the old law and a new heart. So I thought, I'd better hold out and wait. And shortly after I renewed my vows I was told to report to the chancery office. The Provincial met me in one of the reception rooms in the Mother house. She didn't say anything at all. She just handed me an envelope which I discovered later contained $500. Then she said, bitterly but sadly, 'Well, I simply can't believe you're going to go through with this!' "

The Provincial had assembled a train to accompany Sr. Armel to Chancery: the Superior of the house in which she was confined (the woman had never spoken to her), her previous Superior, and a young assistant. It was a glum procession indeed. Her former superior was crying piteously. "When we got to the entry to the chancery, I turned to the Provincial and—I still can't believe I had the courage to do this—I told her one of them could accompany me to the office, but I wasn't going to allow a procession. She was indignant, and told me she had never been spoken to like that before!

"I apologized to her, but said I thought it was demeaning of me to bring all these people to this occasion. She turned to one of her assistants who handed her $100, which she gave to me. 'I wanted you to have this,' she said, somewhat regretfully. I actually wondered if she were trying to bribe me! 'We have to let Mother Alladay go up there with us,' she insisted, and I assented to that—'but no one else!' I said."

She mounted the stairs in the Diocese of New York Chancery on the day she was to sign her dispensation papers. She would thereby relinquish her habit—the only garb she had worn for two decades—and her very name. And, just as daunting, she was forsaking the vows of poverty, chastity and obedience that had guided her for so long. Accompanied by Mother Provincial and her Mother Superior, she entered the offices of Monsignor Joseph Snee, chancellor of the New York diocese. The Mothers Provincial and Superior were distressed by Sr.

Armel's draconian decision, but seemed ultimately to reconcile themselves to what they understood as a deep and fervent longing on Sister's part to serve God in another way.

But Monsignor Snee was not convinced. He was angry. " 'Sit over here and take this pen with which you are going to sign your soul away,' he commanded. 'Sign your passport to Hell.' By now I was shaking, but I signed it, and then I knelt down and said to him, 'Will you please give me your blessing?' He scoffed. 'Blessing? For what you're about to do?' 'But Monsignor,' I said, 'I don't yet know what I'm going to do.' 'I know one thing,' he retorted, ' in six months' time you'll be coming back in that door saying to me, "I made a terrible mistake" ' and he started making pathetic weeping noises. I told him that that might happen, but that I surely didn't intend for it to be that way. Finally, he gave me his blessing. Shaken but resolute, Mae Gintling–Sr. Armel de la Providence no longer–bid her adieus, and walked out into the cold December afternoon and into her new life–whatever that might turn out to be.

In her later years Sr. Mary Elizabeth would recall her work with the Little Sisters with respect but with little enthusiasm. She told about the Mother Superior of the hospital in Baltimore who demanded herculean performances from her assistants. She told of exhausting days filled carrying meals four flights up narrow convent stairs to nuns too old and infirm to leave their rooms, a chore that would leave her breathless and so weary she had difficulty staying awake for evening prayer services. She told of not being permitted to attend her mother's funeral or visit with her family, even though she was in the same city. She said that many years later she had a sudden breakdown and relived her mother's death and finally had some closure to this traumatic time in her young life. However, what most troubled her were her thwarted efforts to help more people in need. But she was convinced that her experience there gave her the strength and wisdom to be a good religious. "I was there for 21 years! I never could have done what I do if I hadn't been with them for so long, and so I am always grateful to them. If I hadn't had hardships with them, it would have been somewhere else because the Lord has to train you someplace. The Little Sisters strengthened me and enlightened me."

She passed through the gates of the convent and recalled the mystical insight she had received months before. "I was frightened of leaving, I must confess. I was fearful that I would be estranged from people outside religious life. I never had a desire to be anything but a nun, never had any interest in associating with people outside. I worried that I wouldn't find a bridge between the two worlds. But the minute I stepped out into the street and into their midst, I felt so much love for each person who passed me by. These were my sisters and my brothers, and in them, too, in each of them, Jesus was being born and was suffering and dying. I easily passed out of one realm where I belonged into another to which I had been called. I felt so blessed by God at that moment.   He showed me that it wasn't going to be impossible to carry out my plan for a new ministry."

"Here I Am, Lord!"

Mae's call, as she understood it, was "to create a little City of God" in the midst of the detritus, human and material, of the American city, among those who dreamed of justice and peace but lived waking nightmares of crime, poverty and decay. But, how to begin? She intended to find a church that would buy three or four city blocks where she could establish that "City" in which an army of volunteers would minister to those in need. She envisioned four or five homes for the aged, four or five for children. There would be a job placement center and a school and a health clinic and a legal aid bureau. And at the center would be the church, home to the volunteers who would devote themselves out of charity and a love of the Lord. "And that Christian charity would be the embodiment of the living mystical body of Christ and it would be lived by everyone in the parish in this little City of God. That was my first plan. I was 50 years old and I was beginning a ministry that was still a mystery to me. I didn't know where to go or what to do. I just went out into the world and said, 'Here I am, Lord!'

" Not surprisingly, Mae Gintling didn't find a pastor who was interested in embracing her colossal plan.

She had left New York and returned to Baltimore for the first time in 22 years, to the inner city where, at 6 years of age, she had had her eyes and heart opened to human suffering. Although her intention was to live in poverty among the poor, she initially moved in with her brother Robert who supported her while she struggled to find her way. In early 1965 she acquired her Maryland RN license and began looking for work that would sustain her while she established her ministry. She met with sympathetic and progressive pastors of inner city churches who, she hoped, would hire her to do home care for their elderly parishioners, work she was quite an expert doing.

Disheartened at finding nothing, she journeyed to Pittsburgh where she hoped to work with Tom O'Brien at St. Joseph's Hospitality House. But she wanted to do more than serve soup to the poor, which was the essence of Tom O'Brien's ministry. From there she went to Philadelphia and decided to live with a group of former Little Sisters of the Poor at the Regina Nursing Center, but left after less than a month, discouraged by the strict rules of life these women had adopted which forbade them from talking to each other except when they were on duty or visiting each other's rooms.

She returned to Baltimore once more. After securing a position with IVNA, a non-profit home health nursing program, she met with Monsignor Austin Healy about starting a home nursing program for inner city families. But the directors of IVNA objected to Mae "moonlighting." She was given the choice of directing the Archdiocesan Inner City Community Health and Human Services program she had founded, or working exclusively with IVNA. Not surprisingly, Mae resigned her post at IVNA. Thereafter she began work as a general duty nurse at Bon Secours Hospital while also providing care for her patients through the archdiocesan program.

Then, in September, 1965, she met with Fr. Donald Knox, CM, at Immaculate Conception Parish, one of the poorer parishes in the city at that time. Fr. Knox was impressed by Mae's vision and her passion for realizing it. He gave her permission to work out of the church's rectory basement. "It's not that great a gift," Fr. Knox told Mae. "I've never been down there, and I've been pastor here for 11 years!" Unused for all those years, the basement was filled with dust and debris. Getting it into usable shape might have discouraged other 50 year old women, but Mae quickly revealed the personal allure and resourcefulness that were two of the signature hallmarks of her work thereafter.

"I had made friends with this young man, Fred Jackson, a teacher at Mt. Carmel in Essex. We might have met in church, I can't remember. But he got his class to come over and clean out the entire cellar and whitewash it for me. It was so filthy, we made the kids shower in the rectory before letting them go back out into the neighborhood because they were covered in soot and coal dust and the grime of years of disuse." A local store gave her linoleum to put over the cement floor, and soon Mae was satisfied that it was presentable for the many people she knew would come to her for help. When she found an old chair and a desk being discarded from a nearby hospital, she was overjoyed and knew that God was watching out for her. As she said many times, "God must be laughing all day long. He does all the work and lets us think we're accomplishing so much." And so, with a clean basement, a desk and a chair, Mae's Joseph House ministry, originally called Josephenium, was officially opened on October 15th, 1965.

The Baltimore Years

Her only personal income those first few months was a $15 weekly stipend she earned working in the Archdiocese offices doing clerical work, and the occasional proceeds from Immaculate Conception's poor box. But despite the hardships, she rejoiced in the freedom she enjoyed to help the poor in whatever way was needed. When Msgr. Healy, who had hired her to work in the diocese office, discovered what she was trying to do, he advised her to quit her job with him and do her ministry full-time. How could she work for the poor if she was spending her time working for a paycheck? He told her she needed to start a mailing list and a newsletter to raise money, but this notion seemed beyond her capabilities at the time. And he told her she could and should use part of the funds to support herself, a concept utterly alien to her until he reminded her that she was one of them, that she was herself living a life of poverty. "So I thought it over and concluded he was right, and so I gave him my resignation. He wished me well, and off I went, jobless!"

"I tell you, it was such an impossible-looking enterprise that nobody wanted to get behind it and encourage me. They thought I'd be defeated in a month or two and didn't want to throw their money away on a thing that would fail. But I never minded that. I always trusted God, and He always came through, that was the great thing."

She told Fr. Knox about her decision to work for the poor full-time, and told him also that she needed a place to live, that she couldn't continue driving back and forth from her brother's house in Essex. A friend had bought her a car, but the gas was just too expensive and would be a needless expense if she could find a place to live near Immaculate Conception. He told her she could use the poor-box money for rent, and he found her a room on the third floor in the home of an elderly couple nearby. As Dan McDonald, one of Joseph House's longest serving resident volunteers wrote, "Lying awake at night, listening to the mice scurrying across her floor, she put her complete trust in the Lord—and a bag of marbles that she'd roll across the floor to keep the mice at bay. She hadn't established the ministry she envisioned, but she vowed that she would willingly go where He led her."

Living with the mice, Mae spent her days raising money, seeking volunteers, buying food and other supplies for distribution, counseling those who came to Immaculate Conception's basement for help, and following a regimen of prayer that strengthened and comforted her as she struggled to do God's will. She gave over 500 talks that first year at churches, schools and service organization meetings, explaining the needs of the poor and begging for money and volunteer assistance. She was often exhausted and occasionally disheartened by the lack of support she got, and she experienced the pain and hardship of being a poor person herself. "Really, I had nothing. Many times I didn't have anything for breakfast or lunch because I couldn't afford to buy anything and was only entitled to the supper Fr. Knox gave me at the rectory."

News of this white woman living alone in the black ghetto of Baltimore began to spread, and small donations trickled in. Unfortunately, Mae also bore the brunt of hatred and prejudice from people who feared what might happen if blacks were able to cast off the shackles of poverty that had kept so many of them "in their place" for almost 350 years. "Racial prejudice was so widespread when I began Josephenium," she said. "Some of the people in attendance at the talks didn't like my message and walked out. One man was so enraged he actually punched me because I was helping poor black people." Meanwhile, in the inner city, she had guns pointed at her and a knife pressed against her throat. She was often frightened, but "I knew the Lord would help me get through these things—and He did."

Cheerfully embracing the poverty of those she served, Mae Gintling came to be loved in the ghetto. Her conspicuous trust in God's providence and her almost palpable love for the poor won people's trust and respect, and taught them the beauty of unconditional love and faith. Eventually, "when I knocked on someone's door and said 'Josephenium,' the door opened right away. They knew I was taking risks for their sake. They respected me for that."

Then one day a prosperous-looking young man appeared at the door of her "offices" in the dank basement at Immaculate Conception. John Delclos had come to help any way he could. He worked at Maryland National Bank, felt a need to share his good fortune with the less-fortunate, and got Mae's address from the Catholic Charities office in Baltimore. They told him about Josephenium, about this eccentric white woman living alone in the ghetto, trying to start a ministry to help the poor. Maybe, they suggested, he could either help her start it or talk her out of it, one or the other.

"When I saw him coming down the cellar stairs, saw those polished shoes and pressed pants and those gold cufflinks and that beaming face that looked as if it had been scrubbed with Ivory Soap ever since he had been born, I thought, now what in Heaven's name am I going to do with him, here in the ghetto, two blocks from the red-light district!"

But, she would say later, God sent just the right person, and just when she most needed him. He immediately began advising her and guiding the business of Josephenium. He helped Mae set up a bookkeeping system to record the donations that were beginning to arrive, and to create the mailing list Fr. Knox had counseled her to assemble. "He undertook all that for me," Sr. Mary Elizabeth recalled fondly. "He was just what I needed." He went with her to visit the poor and sick and elderly people she was now helping on a regular basis. He was uncomfortable at first in the roach-infested rooms, but he cared deeply for the people Mae cared for.

As John spent more and more time with Mae, he became increasingly more prayerful, more spiritual. During his first year the two of them went on a Better World Movement retreat in Washington, and John realized that he had a vocation to become a priest. "So I lost him," Sr. Mary Elizabeth laughs, "but the Church gained a brilliant priest. He became a tremendous retreat master for the diocese, and he brought many more volunteers from the seminary to Josephenium. He was my first volunteer, and I don't know what would have happened to me without him. That was in 1966, I think, before the riots."

"He came to celebrate my birthday with me, my fifty-second, I think it was. He gave me a recording by a violinist he adored. I don't remember the name. I used to play it over and over, since it was really the only record I had! My brother had made me buy the record player on credit, to establish my good credit at the bank, but I was really frightened of owing anyone any money, so I paid off the debt almost immediately—and ruined my credit! John also gave me a box of candy and another very large, heavy present. Inside was a beautiful silver serving for twelve. I was shocked! 'Where did you get this?' I asked him. Turns out he had been engaged, and when he broke off the engagement, wondered what he'd do with the silver set.

'I don't expect to use it,' he told me. 'I'll find out what it's worth and you can sell it and use the money for food or coal.' So I was making dinner for us, and watching John all the while, and wondering where I had seen his face before. And suddenly it came to me. 'Where did you grow up?' I asked him. '23rd Street, in St. Ann's Parish.' My parish! My neighborhood. And then I remembered: his father used to walk to and from work right down our alley! 'Yes, my father and my Uncle Victor,' John said, as amazed by this connection as I was. 'Do you know, I used to watch your father, and my father said, more than once, "See those two men. They're Spanish. They don't fool around like so many of the young men do these days. They go to work and take care of their families. That's what I want my boys to do." '

As John spread the word at St. Mary's Seminary about Mae's work, she began meeting more and more young men who would come to Immaculate Conception to fulfill their weekly service projects. Often she would have eight to ten seminarians going out into the neighborhoods bringing food and comfort and spreading the Word. With these young men she created a nucleus for the work that needed doing. "I used to try to give them supper once a week," she said. "We'd cook whatever came in as donations. Those boys were very good workers."

John became an inspiring priest and teacher, leading retreats and classes throughout the country. "He was a very spiritual person," his friend, Fr. Tom Composto said. "He was the kind of guy who paid attention to the underdogs. He was always teaching, always showing the way." Shortly before his death from cancer in 2007, Fr. Delclos wrote that he wished no flowers at his funeral. Instead, he asked that "people. . .treat a homeless person with love and compassion, and maybe to a lunch or a night (or more) in a hotel."

Soon after John Delclos left for the seminary, an intensely shy young priest, Fr. Joe Breighner, came to work with Mae. "He was so shy, so timid, afraid to come out of himself. He was awkward in every way. When I sent him out on his first solo home visit, I insisted that he wear his [Roman] collar. He came back, very upset, and said that he just couldn't do it. I said to him, 'Joe, you've just got to do it. We need you to do it. I hope you'll go home and think deeply about this. And if you change your mind, come back next week.' He came back," Sister laughed. Joe went on to become one of the more outgoing—and out-spoken--priests in the Baltimore diocese, hosting a country music program, writing weekly columns for The Catholic Review, authoring several books on Christian life and thought, and was one of the leading retreat masters in the Baltimore diocese.

From Josephenium To Joseph House

When she acquired her subterranean office, Mae realized that if she was going to ask people to give her money for her work she'd have to "be somebody," as she put it. She knew she was certainly not going to name the ministry after herself, so she prayed to St. Joseph because he was such a great model of humble care-giving, a simple carpenter and protector of the Holy Family. She promised she would work all her life for the poor if he would provide the money. She told him she couldn't do both, so it was up to him to get the money for her. She also told Joseph that she wanted to name her ministry after him, but it was the Sixties, she said, and it was not an especially opportune time to be outwardly religious. "I remember reading about a seminary in the mid-west called 'Josephenium' and I thought, well, it has the name "Joseph" in it and doesn't use the word "Saint," so maybe I could use that." She had a phone installed and listed it as "Josephenium House," but when a representative from the phone company called one day asking for "Mrs. Enium," Mae knew her choice was a dubious one. "So I said, okay, I can't call it 'Saint Joseph,' so why don't I just call it 'Joseph House?' That's how I settled on the name. I put it on my monthly letters, and the money started coming in. Saint Joseph was doing his part of the job! But I was always unhappy because I couldn't call it 'Saint Joseph.' "

The money came in, and so did the people seeking her help—slowly at first, but as the word spread, more and more came to the basement in the church to tell this white woman their stories. "One day shortly after I opened the doors, I saw this little black boy peeking at me through the basement window. He smiled at me and said, 'Hi, Whitey.' I returned his greeting and he asked, 'You live down there in that cella?' He was about 8 or 9. 'No,' I said. 'Well, watcha doin' down there? Can you get out if you want to?' I told him it was my office. 'Like the principal's office?' he asked, suspiciously. He asked again what I did down there and I told him I looked for people who needed my help. The next day he was back, asking now if he could come down to my office. 'Can I sit in your chair?' he asked, and before long he was curled in the chair sound asleep. He slept the whole day. His name was Derek."

Mae asked him if he had a home, and shortly after that second day, went with him to his house to meet his mother, who told her the boy didn't have a bed, hadn't had a bed in his life. He slept on the floor in a corner because she had a very large family. Mae went to work and found a bed for him at the Saint Vincent de Paul storehouse. Soon afterward, a few more people who had heard about Mae and the bed began showing up at the basement.

By the time John Delclos arrived, the trickle had become a flood, and Fr. Knox told her she'd have to find another place to meet with her clients. The seminarians searched for a house nearby that would give them more room to interview people, but the costs of buying or renting were simply beyond Mae's means. But, as she said, Saint Joseph was always watching out for her. At about this time she was invited to attend the Lafayette Market Association annual banquet and speak to its members who had heard about her and were giving her an award of merit. She gave her speech, and concluded by mentioning somewhat fatalistically that the program for which she was being honored would have to close its doors if she didn't find a permanent location for the day-to-day operation of the ministry. A well-known Baltimore businessman, Arnold Kurland, was moved by what he had learned that day about Mae and her work and without hesitation he offered to rent her a three-storey row house around the corner from Immaculate Conception on McCulloh Street for $1.00 a year. It was to be the first of several Joseph House locations in Baltimore.

In the beginning, Mae would meet with two or three families each day, but she always followed up their visits with a visit to their homes. She discovered quickly that these poor people had learned to get along on their wits, and that they didn't always tell the truth but told her what they thought she wanted to hear. She knew she could learn a great deal by visiting families where they lived, and learned, too, that if this was done in the right spirit, done out of love and concern, the families didn't resent her coming to see them. She said she wasn't afraid at all, even though she found herself in some difficult situations. "I'd sometimes go into a bar and pull a guy out and make him go home to his wife and kids. I was really single-minded!"

The first family that came to her after Derek's visits lived in a large house across from Immaculate Conception. A mother and her nine children lived there. The father was in prison for murder. The family had no money for coal, and the nights were getting colder. Mae enlisted Fred Jackson from Mt Carmel High School to help her carry bushels of coal from a coal yard about three blocks from the rectory. But a bushel of coal, costing fifty cents, would last almost no time at all. The family would need more before the morning was gone. She told Fred she had to find a better way, and with her usual diligence she eventually discovered the Coal Bank that would deliver a ton of coal for twelve dollars.

"Soon I had many people from as far away as the east side of the city coming for coal when they found out I could get it for twelve dollars. One man came and said he didn't have any money but that he would pay me three dollars each month until he got it paid for. This man walked all the way from East Baltimore to the west side where I lived. He came back four times, walking all the way, just to give me the three dollars. He was a little old man. He restored my faith in humanity which was sometimes tested by the deception of a few of the people we helped. I remember, on his last visit, he only had two dollars. He said he'd be back with the last dollar, but I told him not to bother. He had done enough. I thought I was poor then, but he was much worse off than I was."

Of course, there were those benighted souls who merely took advantage of Mae's heart. Years later, Sr. Mary Elizabeth told Ron Alessi, " 'There are people who take advantage of our generosity, I'm sure.' When I asked her how she dealt with that, she said, 'you know, that happens, and you can't let it prevent you from helping those who really need your help. And most of them need help. So, that's going to happen, that's part of life, but you need to keep an eye on your goal, know what your vision is, what your priorities are, and not worry that a few people will swindle you.' "

Mae's infectious warmth, faith, savvy and great good humor attracted a diverse and energetic lot of students, drop-outs, seminarians, VISTA workers, conscientious objectors and retired folks, all united by the desire to live the teachings of the Gospel, all who cared to alleviate suffering in the world. With the help of the seminarians from St. Mary's Seminary and novices from the Franciscan Sisters of Baltimore, idealistic young men and women who revered Mae as a disciple who lived Christ's precepts to love and to serve all of his people, and as a leader of the burgeoning civil rights movement, she refurbished the house on McCulloh Street in a surprisingly brief time, and on May 1st, 1966, the feast of St. Joseph the Worker, Joseph House was opened to the public, to those helping Mae with her endeavors, and those for whom the labor was zealously performed.

Mae swiftly attracted a devoted permanent eight-member volunteer staff who were soon directing a comprehensive array of services for the poor. Besides offering emergency financial assistance for rent and utilities, they provided food supplements, tutoring, foster care, job placement and recreational activities for people of all ages. Developing practices that were the hallmarks of her almost 40-year ministry, Mae probed deeply into the lives of those she helped, trying to discover causes of and resolutions for what kept them imprisoned in poverty. She was forthright and persistent and gentle and often funny. By the time they marked the first anniversary in 1967, Joseph House had helped over 1700 families, and that was just the beginning. To accommodate the growing caseload of families in need, Mae opened a second Joseph House on Druid Hill to continue what she called her experiment in Christian living which set a precedent for continual expansion in order to meet the needs of the poor. This was followed by the dedication of Joseph House East on Lombard Street which Mae opened to serve the Hispanic and Indian populations on Baltimore's east side. Over the next 10 years, thousands more families in need were helped by this small, grey-haired woman's loving but no-nonsense approach with her strong emphasis on helping the poor help themselves. As early as 1970, Joseph House had over 9000 files on individuals and families in need.

❧   ❦

In the summer of 1970 after his first year in college, Tom Anselmi was working as a horse wrangler at Camp St. Benedict run by the Benedictine monks of St. Paul's Abbey near Newton, New Jersey. Fr. Bruno Lawrence, a Carthusian monk from the monastery of the Grande Chartreuse in the high, remote mountains of Switzerland, was visiting St Paul's that summer and the two became friends as Tom pondered what seemed to him his calling to the priesthood. He had a need, he decided, to leave the comforts of college life and do more for others, and he thought this might be the prelude to a vocation. "I'd like you to meet Mae Gintling," Fr. Bruno told him. Bruno Lawrence was, he disclosed, Mae's cousin. They had grown up together in the Gintling home. Bruno's mother had died when he was an infant and his father—Mae's mother's brother—couldn't take care of him. So he became so much a part of the Gintling family that Mae would on occasion refer to him as her brother—and Bruno, "Bo" to the family, would, in his toddler years, call Mae "Mama," much to her consternation. "I had been gone for three years' nursing training and came back and here was this little boy following me around calling me his mama. People thought I had gone away and had an illegitimate child!"

Bruno told Tom about Mae's work with the poor, and when the camp closed at summer's end, Tom went to Baltimore. He knew immediately that this is where he belonged, that he was not going to go back to his little Catholic college near New Orleans, that he had found the place he felt he was meant to be. "I talked with Mae on the phone before I went down," Tom recalled. "She told me she was expecting two conscientious objectors to join her staff of permanent volunteers, and said she thought I'd fit right in with them." Even before I met her, I felt drawn to her and to her work. I got a ride to Baltimore, moved into the Eutaw Street house, and became her driver. Wherever she needed to go, I drove her." In the mornings he helped serve clients at Joseph House, and in the afternoons he'd accompany Mae on her visitations to the homes of those she helped. Many days she would also go to meetings throughout the city to give talks about poverty and Joseph House's efforts to alleviate it.

"My life that year was a bit complicated," said Tom, laughing as he thought back to those youthful days. "I admired Mae so much, and wanted to live as she lived. I was thinking about joining the Paulists because they were out there on the streets, they did the street-front stuff. That's why Bruno told me to spend time with Mae, to see if that was really for me. And I loved it, loved the work we were doing in Baltimore. But I had also met this wonderful girl at college, and I wasn't sure I could live without her. So I stayed at Joseph House for an entire year, and went on a lengthy retreat at Berryville in Virginia, and came back and told Mae that I was going to marry Vicki. Mae was very upset. We had become very, very close. But when summer was over, I left."

Vicki, Tom's wife for more than forty years now,

remembered how difficult that year was. "Mae paid Tom $50 a month, all of which he spent on phone calls to Louisiana, but it was never enough, and I had to beg money from my father, and one month had to sell all my clothes and books to cover a $200 phone bill! And when I would call Tom, Mae would answer and say, 'Vicki, you're not getting him—I'm keeping him!' And I'd say to her, 'Mae, please put him on the phone—I sold all my clothes for this call!'" Vicki is almost wistful, recalling, "I didn't meet her till our honeymoon, actually. Till the end of her life she would tease me, saying, 'Vicki, you have to share him with me.' So that was kind of nice; we both fell in love with the same guy."

"I love Vicki," laughs Tom, "but I never met a person like Mae. She would not take 'No' for an answer. Never, ever took 'No' for an answer to a petition. We'd go out into the white suburbs around Baltimore and she would say, basically, 'I want your money!' And she'd get it! She would have what I can only call visions, and once she had them, they'd become reality. She didn't see barriers. That's what I learned most of all from her. Vicki has always said to me, 'You're like Mae; you never see obstacles.'"

Many years later a neighbor in Salisbury was extolling Mae's virtues, praising the good things Sr. Mary Elizabeth was doing in the community. "He was going on and on about her, about what a difference she was making in the lives of those no one else seemed to care about," recalled Ron Alessi, describing the encounter. 'But,' the neighbor said, 'don't let her get you in a room with the door closed, because you're going to be stuck in there until you give in to her wishes.' " Ron became one of the ministry's most faithful volunteers; as he said, "Being stuck was wonderful." As Sr. Marilyn remarked, "Sister was convinced that she was giving all of us the chance to help others, and for her, that was the whole message of the Bible, the whole point of human life. She was helping us, as she put it, to grow our bank account in Heaven "

Vicki echoes Tom's recollection, but then adds, "But what I loved most about Mae was her sense of humor. We would be in the worst place. Everything seemed to be falling apart, and all of a sudden, without a hint of a smile, she'd make some little comment that would have us all laughing. She had an amazing way of not taking things too seriously. And I think that's how she most influenced my life; that was the best gift I got from knowing her."

Tom remembered how, in her quiet, persistent way, Mae was able to convince donors to give more than they intended and to convince volunteers that they had more to give than they believed. She always worked from a vision, he said, and it was almost impossible to shake her from her quest to realize it. "Alan Amici, the great Baltimore Colts fullback and Baltimore businessman, was one of Mae's most ardent and faithful supporters, and he'd come to the meetings of this little board of directors with other city notables, and I would watch them just melt to this woman, and end up by agreeing with most of her wishes."

Tom hastened to add that he didn't mean to suggest that Mae used people. "She let people work with her, gave them wonderful opportunities to work with her. That was her gift to them. She wanted a soup kitchen. She got a soup kitchen. She wanted a Montessori school, and soon we had a library of books and a building and teachers for a school for the poor children living in the neighborhood."

"But her most amazing feat, I think, happened when we heard that several of the Benedictines from the abbey in Newton had left the monastery and gone to New Orleans. We had lost several of our permanent volunteers around this time, so Mae bought Greyhound tickets for the two of us, and we rode for 36 hours. She met with the monks, invited them to come to live and work at Joseph House—and they did! They were building houses down there, but they left that ministry and came north to be with us. We were there for less than two days, then got back on the bus for the 36-hour ride home. That's how she operated."

But Tom was equally awed by a few of Mae's other schemes to serve Christ. "She started this seven-step program for inmates at the prison in Jessup. I'd drive her there twice a week. She was their teacher, their psychologist, their spiritual advisor. She became very good friends with many of those men. She helped many of them transition back into life in the community. She met a guy on the Baltimore police force and she told him how he could help these ex-prisoners, and he'd come to Joseph House and work with them. She had these tentacles, reaching out into the community, seducing all sorts of people into the work of charity and love. Things just got done, they just got done! I'd drive her out to the prison in this old beat-up Rambler, and one day she started talking about having a store to sell stuff to raise money for Joseph House, and it wasn't long before the trunk was full of religious books and objects that she sold right out of the trunk! The Joseph House gift shop started in that Rambler."

Tom's amazement and devotion are undiminished. He insists she was the most brilliant CEO he had ever met, that she could have run General Electric. "When I was nineteen, I learned the most important lesson of my life from this simple little woman: don't let anything ever keep you from doing what you think is right. Keep your eyes on the goal; don't pay attention to the obstacles."

Vicki admired her absolute love for the poor and her refusal to romanticize them or their condition. She knew their weaknesses and flaws and yet she loved them unconditionally. And sometimes she helped them best by refusing their plea for money or other material things. "She taught us to be counselors, to cut through the con, to follow up interviews with home visits, which were always eye-opening. Often we'd learn that the need was greater than the humble request.

"I fell in love with her because I'd never met anyone so devoted to one thing. And she did all of it, all the labor and organizing and administering, with such peace. Our days were filled with anxiety and agitation and hurry. It was very difficult work, very difficult. But Mae never seemed disturbed by any of that. She knew there had to be enough time because there were always more people to help, and that we'd get it done and do it right. She was always there, pushing us, supporting us, moving us forward. And always there was that sense of peacefulness and calm. She'd sit and talk about children and friends and her dog that she was so madly in love with. She never seemed to worry at all."

"She transformed our lives, and that is no exaggeration. When Tom returned to school, we continued to see each other, and one night, as we were sitting in the car after a date, Tom took my hands and asked if we could pray together. Now, guys have asked me to do lots of things on dates, but this was definitely a first! So, I was expecting a Hail Mary or Our Father, but Tom held my hands and said, 'Thank you, God, for putting Vicki in my life.' And I'm thinking, is this prayer? Are we praying yet? And Tom says, 'God, I want you to lead us.' He finished, and I asked him, 'So, is that, like, a prayer?' And Tom said, 'Yes, Vicki, that's a prayer, that's talking with God.' He had learned that from Mae. Her whole life was a prayer, a communication with God, all day long. She lived her faith every minute, saying, 'God, I'm here, and you'd better be working with me!' Tom learned that from her and he taught me, and I loved it that God was here. She used to say, every day, 'What did you do today to share your faith?' And it wasn't a rhetorical question. We'd spend fifteen minutes or so talking about that."

Vicki laughs, remembering a story she says she loved, a story she thinks is so revealing of Sr. Mary

Elizabeth's character. It happened many years after the Baltimore years, when Tom and Vicki were at Mass with Sr. Mary Elizabeth. "I wanted to introduce her to a dear friend, Fr. Ed Abel, who had celebrated the Mass. As he came toward us, he looked into Sister's eyes, and fell to his knees and asked her to bless him. She was totally taken aback, speechless and embarrassed. She told him to get up, but he wanted a blessing. So she said, 'Okay, God bless you. Now please get up!'"

The larger the ministry became the greater were the numbers of volunteers and the legions of those in need. With growth came new ideas and the expansion and refinement of existing programs. Volunteers offered home-care nursing, marriage counseling, an ex-offender program and adult literacy classes, while students from Mount Saint Agnes and Notre Dame College tutored neighborhood children. They offered a summer bible school for children and a catechetical program for adults. They also cooperated with the Inter-Faith Service Agency to provide a rural summer vacation program for inner city children. Field trips to parks, museums and athletic events were arranged throughout the year.

Mae was clearly a skilled administrator and, more significantly, a canny leader of the ever-growing army she had mobilized (in Fall 1967, 140 seminarians were volunteering their time and skills, and that was just one of the groups working that year). She was undeniably in charge of the ministry but she encouraged her disciples to evolve and expand the mission's myriad programs to correspond with each volunteer's disposition and expertise. In a span of just less than four years, Joseph House had established different enterprises in four separate residences in the inner city. In one, to further help provide for the material needs of the poor, Mae opened Joseph House Thrift Shop. Four neighborhood women ran the shop which sold donated housewares, clothing and furniture at nominal cost to those struggling to provide decent homes for their families. In another building, she began a Montessori School, the Joseph A. Campanella Discovery School, for children from impoverished homes. In another she opened Joseph House Gifts to raise more money and to provide income for the artisans from destitute Third World countries worldwide, a commercial venture that had the added benefit of introducing patrons to the plight of their neighbors near and far. Elsewhere she opened a soup kitchen called Christ Room, and she chaired the organization of a prison education program for inmates in the Maryland House of Correction in Jessup.

In the midst of all this growth, Mae nurtured the spirituality of Joseph House and welcomed the community at large—clients, volunteers, neighbors, the idle and the curious. By means of regular Thursday night liturgies and a weekly seminar series on Poverty and Christian Response, attendees explored the invitation to love offered by Jesus in the Gospel. In the late 1960s and early 1970s, a time of war and protests against war, of assassinations and rioting and violent social and political upheaval, Mae Gintling understood that a deep-rooted faith in God and his love for his creation was the answer to the brokenness, pain, rage and sorrow of all people. Over time a community formed at Joseph House organized around prayer, the Eucharist, service to the poor, and fellowship. Mae was certain that a community which had at its core an abiding love of God provided the foundation needed to carry on the ministry of Joseph House. By 1972, Mae had made clear the direction she wanted to take the ministry. In the January issue of the newsletter she had declared, "From February 1st on, Joseph House will identify itself as a Christian community brought together by the Lord, whose mission it is to incarnate the faith it has in the Person of Jesus Christ and His Gospel. "

Inspiration: Meeting Dorothy Day

In 1966, Mae was invited to attend a special retreat at the Jesuit novitiate in Wernersville, Pennsylvania. There she met Dorothy Day, who had been an inspiration for her for many years. And, she discovered later, they had been the first women to ever stay in that retreat house because it was a novitiate for young men entering the Society of Jesus. She was called to the retreat by Fr. George Anderson who had been a volunteer at Joseph House and before that a social worker with the Baltimore City social service department. "He worked on our staff and was truly a wonderful example to all of us," Sr. Mary Elizabeth recalled. He would use his own small salary to help clients who needed successive payments on things. I remember a young girl who had some talent and some abilities, but who had no money to go to school. So he sent her to school at his own expense, but he made her apply to Joseph House for the money. Then he would send the checks out as if they were from Joseph House. So the girl never knew who was paying for her education. He used to do a lot of things like that."

Fr. Anderson convinced the Father Superior to invite Dorothy Day and Mae Gintling to the novitiate for a series of talks and discussions. "I had known about her and read about her because in my younger days as a nurse I had worked with the Catholic Worker in Baltimore when it first started," Sr. Mary Elizabeth said. "I volunteered there for a short while when I was doing my studies at Mercy Hospital. I had read her writings and had read about her work and I admired her very much. When she came to Loyola to speak I invited her to Josephenium, as it was still called then, and she came. But my first meeting with her was at Wernersville."

Mae deeply admired Dorothy Day's ability to live her life entirely among the poor and to share with them absolutely anything and everything she had. Mae was inspired by Day's refusal to keep anything for herself alone. "She was the poorest person I think I've ever met. When she would leave one of the Catholic Worker houses she was visiting (in Washington or Baltimore or New York and elsewhere), Dorothy would insist that her empty room be used to house the poor. Many times, I was told, she would arrive at a house, and if they didn't know ahead of time and someone else was sleeping in her room, she slept in somebody else's bed, often on a urine-stained mattress. But Dorothy would just lie down in it as if it were her own."

Sr. Mary Elizabeth said that Dorothy Day was the most selfless person she had ever met, and said that she admired that tremendously. Selfless, and so serenely self-possessed, Sr. Mary Elizabeth said.

She seemed to radiate a calm detachment. And she was utterly humble. But she held tenaciously to her beliefs, and she would occasionally exhibit a chastening temper. "I saw her one night put a priest in his place because he was speaking against the teachings of the Church. She was fearless, and she could handle any argument with anyone because she had thought so deeply and completely about things. But as I say, she was simply, totally unattached to and unconcerned about herself, and that's what I loved best."

"She was a controversial figure, so when she spoke at Loyola, the university enlisted bouncers, so to speak. And they almost had to use them because one man stood up and began to attack her work. I think these people were sent by her enemies to heckle her. And this man stood up and asked if it was true that she had been arrested on a morals charge at one time. And she said, quietly, 'Yes, it's true.' But then she said, 'but there's something worse than that.' 'What's that?' he asked. And she said, 'I have just realized that I have two coats in my closet at home and I can only use one.' And I thought, God, isn't she admirable! To say a thing like that in public, and not to defend herself on the morals charge whatsoever, but just simply to say yes, and then that she just remembered that she had two winter coats at home in the closet and she could only wear one. She was a woman of principle, no matter the expense to herself. Never did she come first; she was always last in whatever God's cause was. So that's why I admired her."

Later, Dorothy visited Mae at Josephenium, and knowing how poor Dorothy lived, and knowing also that she lived in a state of undisguised poverty, Mae was apprehensive that her own devotion to cleanliness and order—an effort to set an example for the families who came to her—might lead Dorothy to judge and perhaps even censure the tidiness of Joseph House. "I was really concerned that maybe she would be offended by that. She entered the front door, gazed around, then looked into the little classroom with desks and chairs neatly arranged that we had created in what used to be the living room . And she looked around and said, 'I would give my right arm to have a place like this!' "

Dorothy gave a talk to the crowd of volunteers and community activists who had heard that she was visiting with Mae. When she finished, she retired for the night to a small bedroom in the back where she might enjoy a quiet and restful night. "I went to see if she wanted anything before she retired, and she was sitting in a little rocking chair in her night gown, rocking contentedly back and forth, reading the prayers of the Mass for the next morning. She really was a very holy person, very prayerful and just. Justice was a big thing with her. And justice was a big thing with me and I think that's another reason I liked and admired her so much. I didn't fear poverty as much as I feared injustice for the poor."

The One Thing Needful

Joseph House was, in five short years, no longer the labor of one small, quixotic woman working out of a basement. It was now a city-wide operation which had touched the lives of thousands of people thanks to the charitable contributions from those who had heard about Joseph House from friends or had read a copy of the monthly newsletter Mae had begun publishing in 1967 to solicit donations and to keep benefactors abreast of how their charity was serving the poor. The ministry was, in fact, so large and dispersed geographically and vocationally that Mae was beginning to feel an exhaustion that would assail her sporadically over the next 30 years. She was, she confessed, "burnt out," and one of her jokes in later years was that she was burnt out so many times that she made an ash of herself.

In October, 1972, Mae took the train to New York to meet with Mother Teresa of Calcutta who was visiting one of her convents in the Bronx. Mae had been directing the efforts of several hundred volunteers to serve the needs of thousands of poor people for 8 years. She was 58 years old and was feeling every hour of those 58 years. Her plan was uncomplicated and momentous: simply put, she wanted the Missionaries of Charity to assume responsibility for the operation of Joseph House. Those who worked with her knew Mae could be compellingly persuasive, and she certainly had a credible case to make for her desire. Here was an opportunity for the Missionaries of Charity to expand into another city with great need of their charity, a city where a ministry compatible with their own was already established. Mae would continue to serve in whatever capacity she might be needed, but the overall responsibility would be lifted from her ageing shoulders.

Mother Teresa was sympathetic but unmoved; not only did she decline the offer, but, perhaps seeing in Mae a woman possessed of her own fervent temperament, she advised her to found her own order and get sisters under obedience to her who would devote themselves to share the burden of Joseph House. Mae returned to Baltimore inspired by what amounted to a charge from this saintly woman who was in every way a role model. Mae had, since relinquishing her vows, yearned to belong to a religious order. She wanted to share a sacramental and community life with others.

Her longing for community never wavered and one year after her meeting with Mother Teresa, she was once again on her way north, this time to Boston, to attend a meeting of former nuns called Sisters for a Christian Community where she hoped to meet others searching for a new charism of shared sacrifice and devotion to God.

But Mae was quickly disenchanted with the SFCC organization. According to her, they had no regulations, they had no real community. They came to meet together maybe once every six months or once a year. There was no formation. If anyone wanted to join, even if they had not been in religious life before, they were accepted. All one had to do was fill out an application. Mae knew immediately that this was not what she was looking for.

In Baltimore's Penn Station she joined three other former sisters and travelled with them to the meeting. One of these was Patricia Guidera, a 22 year old former Daughters of Charity sister. She had undertaken her postulate and novitiate formation, but had suffered emotional depletion and had been advised to leave the community. She was devastated by this rejection. Her vocation, she knew early in her life, was to work with the poor. Like Mae Gintling she had heard the call when she was a child. But her parents had made the decision even earlier, that she would be a nun. When she was 2 years old they chose the religious life for their daughter. Patricia had no choice. She had lived a cloistered life throughout her childhood and, when she was twenty, after one year of college, she entered a religious order that cut her off from a family on which she was perhaps unsuitably dependent. The combination of strictness and isolation was too much for her and so she found herself on the way to Boston where she hoped to ally herself with others seeking to serve God by serving the poor.

Patricia's hope was revivified by this older

woman who with quiet animation and humility narrated the history and accomplishments of the Joseph House ministry. They shared the return trip to Baltimore, and by the time they parted at the station, Patricia had decided that she belonged at Joseph House. In April, 1974, Patricia Guidera became a resident volunteer living, praying and working with Mae on Eutaw Place. Privately, the two of them would spend hours discussing the possibility of forming a new order that would combine a deep prayer life with an active apostolate in which, following the injunction of Brother Charles de Foucauld, they could "cry the Gospel" with their lives.

It was in the Midwest—in, she thought, the Cathedral of St. Peter in Chains in Cincinnati—that Sister Armel de la Providence first felt called to follow in the footsteps of Brother Charles. There, in 1963, she was captivated by a portrait of the French hermit priest who lived a life of quiet Christian witness and died a martyr among the Tuareg people in one of the remotest stretches of the Sahara Desert. Sister Armel knew nothing about this man, had never even heard his name, but she felt drawn to that picture in a way that she could not explain except to say that the face, radiating humility and simplicity and love, seemed to be welcoming her to a new way of life.

In her later years, she couldn't recall any details of the painting, but kneeling there before him, she felt changed. She remembered wondering, "Why am I a Little Sister of the Poor when that's who I should belong to?" For reasons beyond reason and sense, she said, "I felt that I belonged to the family of Charles de Foucauld." She wanted to follow the rule of this man, to adopt his spirituality and his philosophy. One of the first things she did after leaving the Little Sisters of the Poor was to buy a life of Brother Charles and read it. Then, as her plans with Patricia Guidera evolved, she visited with the Little Sisters of Jesus in Washington who, she had discovered, lived in accord with Charles's teaching. "We met with their superior and provincial. They were very good to us, very kind. We went every week for several weeks, Pat and I, and studied the writings of their foundress, whatever writings they would give us permission to see. Their foundress didn't want any of her writings to be available to the public until she was dead. So we did a good deal of traveling back and forth to get what we needed."

Mae had in fact been thinking and praying about forming a community even before her meeting with Mother Teresa, even before leaving the Little Sisters of the Poor. So by now, 1974, she was very persuasive about the idea in her quiet, gentle way, Patricia said. She had so many of the details already figured out and was only waiting and hoping for someone to join her to form a community. With an alacrity that seemed precipitate in retrospect, two months after she moved into Joseph House, Patricia and Mae met with Bishop Joseph Gossman, urban vicar of Baltimore. They explained to him that they intended to live by the ideals of simplicity, poverty, love for the poor, love of Jesus in the Eucharist, and faithfulness

**Sr. Patricia Guidera and Sr. Mary Elizabeth Gintling
1974**

to the Gospel and to the Catholic Church. Gossman, impressed by the earnestness of their plea to begin the work of community formation, granted his permission. On July 7, 1974, which is now celebrated as Foundation Day, at Holy Cross Abbey in the Trappist monastery at Berryville, Virginia, Patricia and Mae received the consecrated habits they had chosen for their ministry and became Sr. Mary Elizabeth Gintling and Sr. Patricia Guidera, Little Sisters of Jesus and Mary.

The habit is composed of a simple blue denim shift, blue cotton headscarf and plain wooden cross hanging from a coarse leather thong. "It's perfect!" Mae exclaimed to Patricia, staring at a department store mannequin wearing an orange satin semi-formal evening gown after which they would model their habits. "It has no zippers, no buttons, just a hole to put your head through." Unlike many religious congregations that had been giving up the wearing of distinctive habits since Vatican II, Mae and Pat desired to publicly identify themselves as women committed to living the Gospel. "We wanted to be poor," Sr. Mary Elizabeth said, and "we also wanted our habits to identify our poverty with our vocation." The habits would be a sign that they had embraced the poverty of their neighbors and would reveal their total dependence on Jesus. They didn't want to hide behind their habits, to demarcate their lives from those of others. "We wanted the poor to recognize us and know that we are just as poor as they are." They also believed that the habits kept them from "getting caught up in materialistic pursuits," Sr. Mary Elizabeth added.

They knew they were going to be criticized for choosing to wear habits. This was a during a time when other orders believed habits were a sign of women's subserviant status in the Church, a sign almost of bondage. Sr. Mary Elizabeth never agreed with that judgment. She believed the habit bound her more closely to the Church and to God, not in bondage but in sisterhood.

Crisis In The Community:
The Wilderness Years

Though they had given much thought to their new identities, they found they were somewhat self-conscious and even chagrined by their transformation and returned to Baltimore at night. Sr. Mary Elizabeth later recalled that they were more apprehensive about donning their habits than taking their vows. They sat in their car outside Joseph House for twenty minutes the night they returned from Berryville, uncertain about what their reception would be. They had good cause to be apprehensive. It isn't at all clear how much Mae and Patricia had shared with the ten volunteers who lived with them on Eutaw Place and formed the core of the ministry, or with any of the hundreds of volunteers who worked with them before they took this monumental step. Essentially, what had been for all intents and purposes a lay, even secular, social justice movement was, by their consecration and vows, transfigured into a religious community.

"Our resident volunteers and volunteer staff members were shocked when they saw us," Patricia

Guidera said. "They didn't understand what their place in a religious order would be, or if they wanted a place in it." According to Patricia, the volunteers objected to a ministry that had affiliations with the Catholic Church, or any church. They were committed to the work of Joseph House and the sacred calling that inspired it, but had resisted Mae's desire to establish Joseph House as a religious agency because of what they perceived to be the Church's intolerance and its political and moral conservatism. They knew Mae's faith informed every aspect of her work. They knew she had been a nun, and that she would choose, if she could, to be part of a religious order again. But they resisted her efforts to link their social ministry to the Church.

Years before the founding of the order, Mae Gintling had made clear how crucial it was for Joseph House to be a ministry that above all strove to bring the poor into a closer relation with God, and did not merely provide temporary and emergency relief for mainly material needs. She announced to the various social agencies who sent clients for aid that Joseph House would henceforth "identify itself as a Christian community, brought together by the Lord, whose mission it is to incarnate the faith it has in the Person of Jesus Christ and His Gospel." And, if that were too obscure, she instructed them that "This change of dedication from being a social agency to being a Christian family means that we no longer wish you to refer persons to us on the same basis as you have done in the past. If you believe, however, that any of the persons you interview are desirous of the kind of Christian response that we will offer, then by all means send them to us....We are in no way limiting our service, but rather deepening it to ground its roots firmly in the gospel of the Lord."

Her on-going frustration and resolve can also be detected in a letter she wrote to Archbishop William Borders in 1974: "The long years of dealing with the poor and living in their midst made me aware that what they really needed was evangelization. The majority of the poor that we have served have no acceptable concept of God, of their relationship with Him, and no knowledge of prayer life and the power of prayer to help them achieve personal fulfillment." As she wrote elsewhere, the material help Joseph House provided was not transforming the lives of those they helped. Their clients continued to live lives of dependency and disorder and irresponsibility. If she could change them, bring them to a love of God the Savior, effect a spiritual transformation, in other words, she believed that a transformation of character would follow.

Finally, she addressed directly those devoted volunteers whose lives were so intimately bound up with the ministry of Joseph House. She thanked them all, but pointed out that lately a few had resigned because they could not reconcile their ideas of the community as a loosely organized democratic and unaffiliated assembly with Mae's increasing insistence on evangelization. Speaking for herself and Patricia, she wrote, "We hope within the next year to really begin a life of evangelical poverty, self-forgetfulness, love and evangelization that will require constant self-sacrifice and devotion, a definite commitment and a struggle for the guidance and approbation of the Catholic Church, and a practice of obedience."

These must have been such painful times for Patricia and Mae and all those who had worked so devotedly with them for so many years. It is clear that Mae knew that what she was doing would drive many of their ministry family away. She wanted them all to stay with them, but knew they had to be of one mind and spirit about what they were doing: "Definitely it will be a while before the entire house and everyone in it will need to be involved in the same effort," she wrote to them soon after she took her vows. "In the meantime we invite you to be at home and to continue whatever you are now doing if you feel that to be what you want to do. I have no choice but to do what God calls me to do, and when and how I believe He wants me to do it. If you can be generous enough to help bring this about by carrying on as before while Sr. Patricia and I try to get our new way ready—I feel certain God will bless you for it. If you cannot share the work while we prepare—we will regret it but try to understand. At all events, whatever comes, let us all try to do what we must with as much love, trust and consideration as we can possibly have for one another and part in such a manner as to make it possible to continue to share our various lives and concerns with each other in the future."

She knew almost with certainty what was bound

to happen, and she prayed it wouldn't, but it did. "They knew we were thinking about taking vows, but they didn't think we really would. I could see that it was going to lead to quite a struggle, so I wrote a position paper explaining what we had done and why. I wanted them to know there was no turning back for us now, and to let them know what their options were."

"I told them they had one of two things they could do. 'There's six of you here, and only two of us' I said. We can't do all of this work alone, it has become so extensive. If you want us to stay on for a while and you want to try to get new members and take over Joseph House, we'll give it to you and go someplace else and start over again. But if you don't want to take Joseph House then we will have to disband Joseph House here and take it elsewhere.' They decided that they would not be able to manage without us being there. So little by little they left. It didn't take them long. And they went to other places and did other things. There was no bad feeling about it, but we were sad to lose them and to lose what we had made in the city."

The ultimate consequence of the decision to form the Little Sisters of Jesus and Mary was that Sr. Patricia and Sr. Mary Elizabeth soon found themselves almost entirely alone, most of the staff and volunteers having decided to "move on," as one of the records from that time vaguely expresses it. They struggled to keep all the various services functioning, an exhausting—and, it turned out, impossible–undertaking. Over a three year span that followed, their efforts led to consolidation, cutting back of services and closure of many programs. The Montessori School shut its doors, and the gift shop on Park Ave. closed temporarily before reopening in a more modest space in the residence on Eutaw Place.

And an even deeper struggle was taking place in what was now, despite its appearance as just another row house residence in the inner-city, the convent of The Little Sisters of Jesus and Mary. How to balance the often overwhelming amount of work required of them, and their need for prayer and meditation? How to achieve a balance between helping the poor and developing a sustaining religious life? A pamphlet published in those early years gives some sense of their lofty goals and reveals also the nature of the contest between these two equally important and necessary elements in their lives. They list among their purpose their intention "to be contemplative in prayer and yet totally given to the spread of the Kingdom through evangelization of our brothers and sisters, meeting them where they are and walking with them to the greatest unity God desires of them." They wanted the community they had established "to be free, detached, people of deep prayer and silence, yet totally sensitive to the concerns and spiritual needs of all our brothers and sisters." They wanted to combine opportunity for retreats, days of prayer and periods of solitude with their endeavors to provide spiritual and material support for the afflicted, the sick, the dying, and all those in need. The effort to achieve this balance would prove to be ongoing in the order and would lead to tension and eventual ruptures that afflicted its members from the very beginning. As one of the resident volunteers in Salisbury described this transitional time, those were "the wilderness years."

A New Beginning

These two devout and devoted women now had to face the reality that their ministry was collapsing around them. They had lost their large staff of volunteers but the numbers of those in need of their aid kept growing. Donations continued to flow into the treasury and flow out almost immediately. Sr. Mary Elizabeth continued to write the newsletter, continued to give hundreds of talks each year to raise awareness and funds. Sr. Patricia served as sole administrator of this gargantuan operation. Both of them continued to interview families seeking help, visiting those who couldn't come to Eutaw Place. "It was too much," Patricia Guidera, no longer a nun, said in an interview. "Too much for the two of us. We worked sometimes 14 hours a day for days at a time. We might not see each other till late at night and were then so exhausted that there was little time for devotions. We were both exhausted and disheartened because we didn't feel we were adequately serving those who came to us."

The nuns also endured the fear arising from being two women living alone on the mean streets of Baltimore. "We lived on what was known as

Prostitute Row," Patricia said. "There were iron bars on all the doors and windows. They were overwhelmed, and occasionally talked about relocating and beginning over on a less punishing scale. As early as 1975 they traveled to Buffalo, New York, in hopes that there they might find a more congenial location for their convent and their work. Nothing came of that visit, and so they muddled along for another year in Baltimore.

In September, 1976, a sympathetic friend, Sam Hill, gave them the keys to his summer cottage in Ocean City, Maryland so they could enjoy a brief respite away from the ceaseless demands they faced each day in the city. They loaded the car for the weekend get-away, and Sr. Mary Elizabeth insisted they take stock from the gift shop that was now closed for lack of volunteers and consequent loss of customers. She could not have explained even to herself why she did it, but in retrospect she knew that God once again had a hand in guiding them where He wanted them to go.

Mae Gintling had visited Ocean City at least once before. Ron Alessi tells the story of a young social worker Mae had met in the ghetto in Baltimore who had a car, and who asked Mae if she'd like to go to the beach for a quick vacation. This social worker, later an ardent volunteer at Joseph House, was Barbara Mikulski, now the senior United States Senator from Maryland, and, it turned out, she had an ulterior motive for her offer. As the two women approached the Bay Bridge, Barbara told Mae she was afraid to drive over the bridge—a fear she shares with more than a few travelers, it seems. "Mae had never driven across the bridge, but she took the wheel without hesitation, and on they went across the Eastern Shore to the sands of Ocean City."

In the Fall of 1976, Sr. Mary Elizabeth and Sr. Patricia settled into Sam Hill's vacation home and went to the Boardwalk. It happened that their vacation coincided with one of the many boardwalk festivals for which Ocean City is known—this one called "Save Six for September." As Ron Alessi told it, as Sr. Mary Elizabeth strolled past the many vendors selling their wares, she instantly saw a chance. First she asked someone, "How do you get permission to do that?" She was told that she needed only to bring a table and her goods and conduct business "We can sell some stuff here!" Sr. Mary Elizabeth told Sr. Patricia. "She had the instincts of an entrepreneur," Ron Alessi said. Their vacation turned into a weekend of work that was profitable beyond their expectations. "Maybe we should move here," Sr. Mary Elizabeth mused. They both knew it was only a matter of time before they would have to close their Baltimore missions. "We knew there was a need for our work on the Shore that was more crucial in some ways than Baltimore because there were so many other programs to help the poor in the city," Patricia explained. "We decided that we could open a shop in Ocean City, work in it during the summer, then use the profits to help people in the Salisbury area during the winter."

They returned to Baltimore with renewed enthusiasm for the ministry which had nearly defeated them. They spent the next nine months closing the Baltimore ministry, what must have been a traumatizing undertaking for Sr. Patricia and Sr. Mary Elizabeth, for the volunteers and donors, and especially for the families who had relied on their help for the past 12 years. The following June, they rented shop space in Ocean City and named it Joseph House by the Sea. They continued to work out of their rooms on Eutaw Place, commuting from the beach to Baltimore. But their presence and effect was much diminished. Though they maintained a residence in the city, a rental on Lombard Street, they also rented a trailer in Ocean City and in 1978 they put the two houses on Eutaw Place up for sale. They would not re-establish a permanent presence again in the city for ten years. So, gradually, inexorably, the two sisters transferred their energies to work with the needy families of Maryland's Eastern Shore. Almost immediately they became aware of the appalling living conditions borne by many residents of this semi-rural region. When they had any free time they explored the quiet country byways branching out from Ocean City and from Salisbury where they observed shocking examples of poverty and deprivation. Too many people lived in shacks without indoor heating or plumbing. They drank rusty water from spigots stuck into the ground. Often these impoverished families lived isolated from others, estranged from a supportive community. Often they were estranged from God. The lack of work, the exorbitant rents charged by landlords, the absence of public transportation to ferry them to places where they might find work and to places where they could get medical assistance kept many trapped in a dehumanizing snare of poverty. As Sr. Mary Elizabeth artlessly explained it, "we took our store to the seashore, worked there in the summertime, and in the winter drove around on the Shore helping the poor where we found them. Until the Lord sent us more sisters, that's how we worked it."

The move to the Eastern Shore was not without its difficulties. "People wouldn't speak to us," Sr. Mary Elizabeth said. "They were prejudiced toward black people and toward Catholics." The nuns lived in a trailer because landlords were unwilling to rent to nuns. Furthermore, citizens of Salisbury and smaller towns nearby were insistent that there was no poverty there. But that was because the poor were invisible to them. "We saw poverty that had to be seen to be believed," Sr. Mary Elizabeth said. "We visited families living with no heat or indoor plumbing—and they were paying outrageous amounts to rent these places. In one warehouse, eight families lived in windowless cubicles. Every 20 minutes the landlord would pump fresh air in. These people—children, elderly, unemployed young people trying to take care of their families—were so miserably hot that they went about virtually naked, sweat pouring off them." Sr. Patricia and Sr. Mary Elizabeth visited a poor elderly couple who were too feeble to care for themselves. "The weeds were so high we couldn't find the door at first. Chickens roosted in the light fixtures and laid eggs on the refrigerator." Sr. Mary Elizabeth said she hadn't seen this level of neglect toward the poor in Baltimore. "In the city, people have more access to agencies to help them and the citizens there are more aware of the poor and more inclined to offer assistance." The more time they spent on the Shore, the clearer it became that they had been sent by God to help people who suffered from what seemed to the two nuns as shocking indifference.

Sr. Mary Elizabeth and Sr. Patricia lived in a trailer, then in the home of a couple that had befriended them at the beach, then in a house they bought and quickly sold because of the health risks they experienced living there. They moved into the Salisbury home of another friend they had made at the beach. They worked ten hour days at the shop, then drove to Salisbury to rest in preparation for the next day's challenges. Somehow, they also found time to visit the overlooked and discounted. They would load up their ageing station wagon with donated goods and items they purchased with the proceeds from the store, and drive out into the countryside, delivering bread, canned food, fresh water, kerosene, wood, coats, shoes, even second-hand stoves. Eventually, they couldn't keep up the pace. The word had spread about the goodness of these two women and of their genuine love for the poor, for these people desperate to feed their children and pay their rent and acquire the most basic goods that, for them, were extravagances.

They needed a more permanent home for Joseph House, and in late 1978 they signed a lease on what became the order's convent and which has served that purpose for 35 years. After what seemed like years of wandering and dislocation and uncertainty about how and where they were being called by God, they moved into a spacious 100 year old home in Salisbury. Now they had the space they needed to provide services to those who had begun to seek them out without waiting for the nuns to come to them. The sisters interviewed their new clients in the first floor rooms, including the chapel they had consecrated and which contained the Holy Eucharist. "We did interviews in the living room, counseling in the chapel, and conferences in the bathroom," Sr. Mary Elizabeth declared, laughing. They strove to unravel the contorted stories people told to explain their distress, their indigence. They knew that some people suffered because of their own weakness and folly, and they had honed their capacity for discernment so they could help those who needed not only material but spiritual support. They sought ways to assist people find ways to help themselves wherever possible, to break themselves out of the cycle of poverty that had imprisoned them, often for their entire lives. But in everyone who came to them, they saw the suffering Christ whom they loved without limit, and for whom they were impelled to action with ceaseless zeal.

Crisis Precedes Transformation

As news of their ministry spread, the impoverished arrived in greater and more desperate numbers. They appeared all day and into the night. They needed food and clothing, help with rent and bill payments. Now no one could maintain that there were no poor in the area. They crowded into the convent and clogged the narrow residential streets. They traveled most often on foot, or drove or were driven in from the country from neighboring Delaware and Virginia.

The crowds flocking around the convent irritated not a few of the sisters' neighbors. Some were clearly repelled by the sudden appearance of so many poor, mainly minority people the nuns attracted by their ministry. Some who lived nearby were running out of patience outside while the sisters were running out of room inside, for although Sr. Mary Elizabeth's leadership and determination frightened some people, it also attracted others, and she began to recruit a host of volunteers and benefactors who took over every unoccupied corner in the convent for their work.

Finally, the neighbors complained about the

congestion and noise and what some saw as undesirable elements. They went to the city council with their concerns, and a representative from the mayor's office visited the convent to instruct the sisters to "cease and desist" their work. The ordinarily composed Sr. Mary Elizabeth was indignant, and informed the mayor that if they weren't helping the poor with their problems, then someone else—perhaps the mayor's office itself—would have to replace Joseph House as provider for the needy. She also made sure that the local media knew about the discord. Very quickly the mayor retreated from his decree, and assured Sr. Mary Elizabeth and Sr. Patricia that he wanted to work with them, not against them.

The mayor's office offered help with controlling congestion and mollifying the grievances of some neighbors, but it was clear to everybody that the ministry had outgrown the convent and that finding another location was crucial if the ministry to the poor were to continue. But there was no opportunity to do anything about the crisis for almost five years, and the poor kept coming.

Fortunately, donations kept coming, too, and volunteers, and benefactors. The publicity Sr. Mary Elizabeth garnered from the confrontation, the newsletter Sr. Patricia wrote and mailed each month, and word of mouth spread the news about Joseph House. "We depended on the goodness of hundreds of people on the Shore who gave us $10-$20 each month," Sr. Mary Elizabeth said. "Sometimes we didn't have enough to meet the needs of the people we served, but I always counted on God to provide what we needed, and He never let me down." To Sr. Mary Elizabeth, everything began and ended with the love of God and the need for people to know and love Him. She would work tirelessly to remind everyone—the poor, the volunteers, the benefactors and donors—of their need to rely on God.

And God always heeded her pleas, she would tell you. In 1979, a young woman entered the store at the beach and before the year was over, Anne Rut-kauskis became the first new member of the Little Sisters of Jesus and Mary since its founding in 1974. Why was it so difficult to attract women willing to join them in their ministry? "It was too hard," Patricia said simply. "Too hard. There was too much work to do. We had the store; we had more and more people seeking help; we had the books to keep, correspondence to keep up with, the newsletter to write and mail. It was too much. And all the time we were desperate to find time for prayer together and alone. A few women considered joining, but they couldn't because they wanted more emphasis on the religious life and that had to mean less on the work of serving the poor. This had been a problem since our days in Baltimore, but for Sister Mary Elizabeth there was never a conflict between work and prayer. For her the work of social justice was prayer, and she was tireless, a workaholic, really. So I thought it was a miracle when Anne became a postulant."

Anne was the second of many women eventually attracted by Sr. Mary Elizabeth, by her zeal and humility and caring heart, and by the kind of work the Little Sisters were doing. And then God answered another prayer—finally, in 1983—when the mayor, working with local philanthropist Bill Riordan and banker David Rodgers, convinced Campbell Soup Company, a major Eastern Shore employer, to "rent" the sisters two large trailers and a warehouse behind their factory for $1.00 per year. Jim Berrigan, another close friend of Elizabeth's (and brother of Frs. Philip and Daniel Berrigan, SJ, conspicuous anti-war and social justice activists and one-time members of the Baltimore Joseph House Board of Directors), set immediately to work with a volunteer crew he assembled from various churches nearby, transforming the warehouse into a clean, comfortable, welcoming help center. On Valentine's Day, 1984, the sisters, volunteers, local ministers and other dignitaries gathered to celebrate the opening of the new Joseph House Crisis Center. The squat, square, unprepossessing cinder block building quickly became a tangible symbol of the concern and involvement of the sisters and the community of helpers they had attracted to help improve the lives of the neediest among them.

Here they had space for private interviews, storage rooms for food and clothing, a dining room where the hungry could get a meal, and a kitchen from which meals were served by volunteers from several churches. They also instituted a Payee Program whereby money received from disability, Social Security, welfare and other sources was deposited and dispersed by Joseph House to pay rent and other bills for clients who were unable to handle their finances, and, in later years, a Good Neighbors program wherein volunteers visited homebound clients, did errands for them, helped them bathe and exercise and generally befriended these people who may not have many friends.

The long lines now trailed away from the Crisis Center's front door from which an estimated $600,000 was disbursed each year, and from the trailers from which upwards of 500-600 bags of food were distributed each day. "When Sr. Mary Elizabeth told me about her plan to open the Crisis Center, I thought she was crazy," said Father Dan McGlynn, who became the sisters' chaplain in 1982 and, later, Sr. Mary Elizabeth's spiritual director. "Of course, this wasn't the last time I'd tell her that," he laughed. "I'd tell her that many of her grand plans were hare-brained and outrageous, and she'd laugh and agree with me and say, 'But it's what God wants me to do!' And she always succeeded where I think others would have failed, and so she convinced me that she was indeed chosen by God to fulfill His will."

With the new center to work from, the corps of volunteers expanded, and services for the poor once again flourished as they had in Baltimore. From financial help for rent, utilities, and anything that might improve the quality of life, to clothing, food, employment counseling, legal help, a warm meal, and friendship, the community of Joseph House endeavored to bring witness of Christ's love to a small town on Maryland's Eastern Shore. In their efforts to live the Gospel of Christ, Joseph House became a corporeal sign of the presence of a loving God. All this work of God began with the decision of one woman, in 1965, to go into the inner-city mean streets of Baltimore, to live with the poor as one of them, and to bring the good news of Christ's love through deeds, not words. Twenty years later, at 70 years of age, she was still laboring in the vineyard for the least of God's children, and would continue her ceaseless ministrations for another 20 years.

Sr. Mary Elizabeth Gintling: A Group Portrait

Who is this woman? We have witnessed what she has done, has accomplished until now. But do we have a true, an accurate portrait of the person she was? Those who lived and worked with her have provided a collective depiction that captures the complexity and even seeming contradictory details of Sr. Mary Elizabeth's character. And as helpful as their observations can be, as penetrating and discerning as their insights into the character of Sr. Mary Elizabeth often are, what we learn about them, about the kinds of people who made up the community surrounding her and who were drawn to devote their lives to the ministry she invited them to live, is equally revealing of Sr. Mary Elizabeth's heart, soul and mind.

Sr. Marilyn, Sr. Mary Elizabeth's closest companion in her last years, entered the Little Sisters in 1990. She recalls Sr. Mary Elizabeth as a tender but tough leader. "She would lecture the interviewers in the Crisis Center all the time: 'You're too soft a touch! You have to learn to listen with real discrimination. These guys will run circles around you if you're not careful!' " Of course the worst-kept secret at Joseph House was that the softest touch of all was Sr. Mary Elizabeth herself. According to Sr. Marilyn, Sr. Mary Elizabeth wanted to give assistance wherever such aid would help the client help herself. "She wanted to do whatever she could to cultivate a spirit of independence and responsibility, so that those receiving help could turn around and help others."

Sr. Marilyn had read about Sr. Mary Elizabeth in the Catholic Extension society's magazine. In 1989, Sr. Mary Elizabeth had been honored by this national Papal society as the winner of its annual Lumen Christi ("Light of Christ") award honoring individuals or groups whose works shine the light of faith on their faith communities. Marilyn was immediately drawn to the woman and her work. "I visited the convent from Minnesota, stayed in one of the rooms always available for guests. The next day, Sr. Mary Elizabeth said they were having a staff meeting and asked if I'd mind taking minutes. Then I was encouraged to take one of Sister's beloved dogs for a walk." Marilyn was overwhelmed by how quickly she was accepted into the community, and how at home she felt in those first hours. After her first conversation with Sr. Mary Elizabeth, Marilyn wanted to become a resident volunteer, but Sr. Mary Elizabeth hastily quashed that plan, and Marilyn found herself making arrangements to enter the order of Little Sisters of Jesus and Mary.

"I never moved so fast in my life," Sr. Marilyn says, reflecting on those early days. And it was all because of Sr. Mary Elizabeth. "I was kind of awed by her, I think. When she looked at me I felt embraced by her spirit. And her look revealed her soul. She had a wondrous smile; she radiated such warmth. I felt like I was being invited to live life in a way I hadn't lived before." She had this huge, deep laugh, Sr. Marilyn recalled. And for all her almost mystical spirituality, she exuded a robust earthiness. "She was a woman of the deepest faith in God's love for us all. She was utterly undaunted by great and little things because of that faith. It was easy for me to make my decision," Sr. Marilyn mused. "How quickly she draws you in," she said softly, as if Sr. Mary Elizabeth were still there, luring others into a life of joyful sacrifice. And, in a real way, she is: her spirit permeates the vast ministry she left behind.

Sr. Connie Ladd, who replaced Sr. Mary Elizabeth as the Mother Superior of the order in 2002, first visited the convent in Salisbury in 1986. She was a divorced mother of two grown children and wanted to make a firmer commitment to the kind of pastoral work that she was doing while teaching full time in Baltimore in what she labeled "the inner-city war zone." A retreat director gave her Sr. Mary Elizabeth's phone number. "She wrote a letter welcoming me for a visit, and included a picture of herself canning beans. I thought, that's not the kind of ministry I had in mind!"

Nonetheless, Connie was touched by the "Welcome Connie!" banner the nuns had hung in the convent. After settling in, she went with Sr. Mary Elizabeth into the quiet yard behind the convent and asked her if, being a divorced woman with two children, she could enter the religious life. "'Do you love the poor?' she asked me. 'Are you a Catholic?' I answered yes to both questions. 'You sure can be a nun, then,' she declared. That night at dinner, I slipped my shoes off under the table, and Sr. Mary Elizabeth's beloved dog, Ziggy, ate them. For Sr. Mary Elizabeth, that was a sure sign that I was one of them!" Next morning, Sr. Mary Elizabeth padded into Connie's room in her pajamas. 'How do you like your coffee?' she asked. This beats the Sheridan! I thought. But there was nothing unusual in her doing that. She was a true and devoted servant of us, of all."

"I visited again that summer. I lived with the sisters for a month, praying with them and working with them at the Crisis Center. Sr. Mary Elizabeth wanted me to help clients find jobs. I had never done any such thing, so I went to the library, got a huge stack of books about employment, and began to study. Sister saw me poring over the books and asked what I was doing. When I explained, she said, 'You don't need books.' At the center the next day, she got a trash can from the soup kitchen, turned it over in the waiting room and pushed two chairs up to it facing each other. On the can bottom she placed a yellow legal pad. 'This is your desk; this is your office. Now, let's find some work for these folks!' "

The "folks" looking for work most often had no phone; many had no address. But Sr. Mary Elizabeth knew how to track them down. "She took me to a house on Fitzwater Street, and I was so shocked by what I saw, I asked God to forgive me, to forgive me for not knowing how terrible were the lives of so many people. This woman lived with her two little children in an "apartment," no more than a single room, with a mattress on the floor and a fan for circulation, bags of food and clothes strewn around. This was in the 1980's! And lots of angry people in Salisbury denied there was poverty and accused the sisters of causing unrest!"

Sr. Mary Elizabeth was always finding ways to awaken Connie to the burden and blessing of complete and utter dedication to serving the poor. There was never too much work, too many people needing help. "She definitely had her favorites—many, many favorites, actually. For example, she was always looking after this one woman—we'll call her June—and Jim, her son born after June had been raped in a mental institution. Because of her disability, June couldn't live with others. One day Sister said to me, 'It's Jim's birthday; we have to get him tennis shoes.' So off we went to Sears to get Jim's shoes. 'I just love to come here,' Sister said as we walked the aisles of the store. 'I love looking at all the things I don't have to buy,' she said, smiling happily."

"After a few experiences like this that summer, I knew I had found my vocation."

❦ ❧

Monsignor Dan McGlynn, pastor of Holy Family Church in Dover, Delaware, seems to know intimately the comforts and hardships bequeathed to those wholly assured of God's love. He listens intently and responds thoughtfully to one's questions. In his discourse and manner he conveys intelligence and humility, kindness and probity. His homilies declare the love of God for all creation and one feels certain that only through prolonged struggle has he come to trust so utterly in this redemptive promise.

Father Dan first met Sr. Mary Elizabeth in June, 1982, shortly after he was appointed to serve as associate pastor at St. Francis de Sales Church in Salisbury. One morning he was surprised by Sr. Mary Elizabeth who had followed him into the sacristy after weekday Mass. Would you, she asked, be willing to say Mass at our convent? Let me check with the boss, he replied. Not long afterward she had scheduled him for talks with the nuns and for hearing their confessions after she had learned that he had a degree in pastoral counseling. He wasn't aware that he was to become their chaplain, "but obviously that was Sister's plan," he laughs. Soon he was leading days of prayer—whole days—at the houses of her friends, and later Sister began to seek him out to counsel her about her leadership of the order. "Much of what we studied was practical stuff--theories of religious life, Church history, active listening skills, addiction recovery —not philosophy or theology. Pretty pragmatic stuff. Sister did formation days, taught them what the vows mean."

When his 5 years at St. Francis came to an end, in 1987, he knew he had to leave and he knew that Sr. Mary Elizabeth didn't want him to leave. "It was pretty clear that the bishop wasn't going to assign me to my new post to satisfy Sr. Mary Elizabeth's desires. But she went and met with the bishop anyway, and somehow convinced him she needed me. She was just so forcefully persuasive; she could get anything she wanted, at least it seemed that way to me." The bishop allowed him to serve as the order's chaplain no matter where he was stationed in the diocese. He would have one day a month to spend with them. He's been meeting with them for 30 years. Over those years he also became Sr. Mary Elizabeth's spiritual director. She would talk with him about the order and share with him what he termed "her hare-brained, outrageous ideas"—like buying the building from Campbell Soup for $1.00 and turning it into a Crisis Center or starting the Village of Hope and the Princess Anne novitiate. He would laugh at her and she would laugh, too. They became close friends, and he would tell her she was crazy and she would agree, but say that God wanted her to do these crazy things.

As she got older she told him she needed him to take spiritual care of the sisters in the order. He told her he loved her and loved the nuns but that he couldn't take responsibility for the order after she died. He would remain as their chaplain but she wanted him to guide the order because he knew how she felt about so many things. He could keep them in the charism. She was worried that the sisters wouldn't be able to function without her or him. "But then she would get quiet, and say that if God wanted the work to continue, it would."

Fr. McGlynn worried about the order and the need for nurturing the sisters in their faith and commitment. "I told Sr. Mary Elizabeth on many occasions that their life in the order should consist of Ministry, Community and Individuality. These were like three legs of a stool, and if one was shorter than the others, the stool could not stand." And, too often, life in the convent was unbalanced. There was much too much emphasis on ministry, sometimes to the ignoring of the two other crucial elements in their lives. There was simply not enough time devoted to care of the individual sisters, or to their relationships with one another. "Sr. Mary Elizabeth was a doer. For her there wasn't time to learn about one's life—there was too much to do. She was so committed to the poor. She believed everyone was sent to her by God. She would teach the sisters on their time off, so she did devote time to the community, but she didn't understand the modern woman's needs who came into the order from different life experiences—widows, divorcees, grandparents, and so on. She didn't understand how much time they needed for formation. There was never enough time for prayer and contemplation. One consequence of this is that few new women entered the order. In my estimation this was a significant mistake."

"Another problem was that she held everything to herself, wasn't grooming anyone to replace her. No one knew about the finances. The other women would never challenge her. Sr. Connie's challenge to her authority when she convinced her that the homeless men needed overnight shelter from the winter storms was a courageous thing." Then they all had a fright: Sr. Mary Elizabeth was on a flight to Houston and the plane had to be diverted because she had a heart attack. This was a wakeup call. No one knew where the insurance policies were; no one knew much about the administration of the order at all. Even in the beginning Sr. Mary Elizabeth wouldn't let Fr. Dan get too close. But then one day he asked her, what will this order be like in 5 years? Be realistic. What will you do as you age, as the volunteers age, and the donors age? Sr. Mary Elizabeth was, everyone acknowledged, the charismatic force that brought new sisters, laymen and lay volunteers in. "Now that Sr. Mary Elizabeth is gone, the Little Sisters of Jesus and Mary are part of the fabric of Salisbury and they are taken for granted. Their challenge is to become visible, to attract all sorts of attention—new members, volunteers, donors. They have to do something to gain attention, to be concerned about growth." He paused and said, almost to himself, "Maybe it will turn into a lay ministry."

Fr. McGlynn came to Salisbury once a month and had communal meetings and classes and celebrated Mass at the convent. And he would meet privately with Sr. Mary Elizabeth, and would interrogate her, trying to get her to understand what needed to be done if the ministry were to thrive after she was gone. What about your funeral arrangements? he'd ask. Who will be in charge when you're gone? He told her she had to retire and that they needed to have an election. Finally, she relented. "Sr. Connie was elected superior general but Sr. Mary Elizabeth was still running the show. Bishop John Barres from the Allentown diocese came and did an audit and told them what they had to do for the succession." It was clear that Fr.McGlynn would challenge her when others could not.

"For Sr. Mary Elizabeth, there was no conflict between her religious life and her ministry. Her shortcoming was she thought everyone was like her. She was there for dinner, for prayer, and could do all that plus the work with the poor. The other sisters couldn't do that. How do you do it all? And if you can't, what is primary? If we don't have community we won't last to do our ministry with the poor. I told her over and over that prayer life and community have to come first or there won't be work with the poor. We would talk about how Mother Theresa had such a great sense of the importance of prayer life. Sr. Mary Elizabeth just didn't have it." She might have had for her personal motto that phrase of the Benedictines: 'ora et labora'–prayer and work. But for her, it seemed, the formulation was the more earnest, more Victorian 'laborare est orare'–work is prayer.

"She had such remarkable trust in Divine Providence. She would often say that sometimes it's not until you come up to the starting line and put your foot in the block that God provides you with the help you need. You can't sit around thinking about doing things, she'd say. You've got to get into the race. Then he will help you. If you're willing to do his work, even if you don't have any money or support. She was secretly proud that she never went into debt, never had a mortgage. The support she needed for the work would always come in.

"She was so creative. She was a visionary. Where we saw an empty warehouse or a neglected country house, she saw the Workshop and the Novitiate. She had so many talents. She was fluent in French; she was a very astute businesswoman; she had an excellent eye for art, for beauty. But for all that, she was an utterly humble servant of the Church, and unlike other leaders of religious orders in the modern Church, she was fiercely respectful of Church authority. She never did anything for which she didn't have permission—even if, often, she would beg permission after the fact." Monsignor McGlynn laughs fondly, recalling one of Sr. Mary Elizabeth's more rascally adages: 'It's sometimes easier to ask for forgiveness than to get permission.'"

Sr. Mary Joseph. When Lois Reinke was 9 years old her mother was hospitalized with a nervous breakdown. Five years later, her mother died of heart failure, never having left the hospital. Lois and her three siblings had been allowed to visit her each month, but their mother was unresponsive to their presence. It was, Sr. Mary Joseph remembers, like visiting a stranger. Her father was a stern but loving parent for his motherless children. He was very strict and had firm ideas about how his children were to conduct their lives. Sr. Mary Joseph recalls being anxious many nights when he returned home from work, and wanting to spend the night with her girlfriend's family.

"One night Daddy announced that he wanted to have a 'serious talk' with us. He told us, 'I have always prayed that one of you would dedicate your life to God.' I stealthily nudged my brother's knee beneath the table as if to say 'You!' I knew I wasn't being called—or so I thought."

Earlier in their young lives, Lois and her sister had promised one another that if either of them became a nun, the other would follow. Ten years later, as 19-year old Lois was boarding a flight to Peru to become the only American in a native religious community, her sister was making plans for her wedding. Lois, who was supposed to be her sister's maid of honor but instead became Madre Maria Josepha and never regretted her sister's change of heart or her own decision to dedicate her life to Christ and the Church.

The community that Lois joined in 1962, The Missionaries of Jesus Word and Victim, served indigenous villages in the Andes of Bolivia and Peru. She loved her mission in South America, loved the stark simplicity of the place and the people, the silence of the world in the high mountains. "We lived in pre-fabricated convents or old abandoned rectories, residing and working where there were no priests or doctors to minister to the physical and spiritual needs of poor farmers and shepherds and their families. At one time I was responsible for the pastoral work in five distant parishes. We baptized, led in the Liturgy of the Word, helped these humble, mostly illiterate people reflect on God's love, distributed communion, trained catechists, prepared and witnessed marriages (the couples administered marriage to each other); we delivered babies, cared for the sick and dying, and buried the dead. The people called me 'Senora Padre!' "

"With the help of Queshwa-speaking guides who brought mules and a donkey for supplies, two of us would travel from village to village, leaving our mother house for two to three week journeys into the mountains. In each village a family, despite their poverty, would take us into their little huts and generously care for our needs."

Sr. Mary Joseph also travelled back to the United States every five or six years for vacations and to visit parishes to raise money for the mission work in the Andes. "One time I wrote to the bishops of all the dioceses in the United States to find those who would give me permission to speak in their churches." Seven dioceses, including Brooklyn, San Antonio and Orlando, welcomed her. "I got a lot of money on that trip," she laughs proudly, "but what I will always remember are the families and convents that took me in, just like the families in

Bolivia and Peru. These people do God's work so easily, so joyfully!" She thought of those days with obvious gratitude. "It was a joyful fulfillment of Jesus' promise that those who leave their homelands, their fathers and mothers, sisters and brothers, will have a hundredfold of lands, fathers and mothers, sisters and brothers. They will always find that welcoming Christian family!"

As the years passed, Sr. Maria Josepha became more and more frustrated by the restrictive rules of the convent life of her community. She found it increasingly difficult to fulfill the obligations of the Rule and also to do justice to the many demands of her pastoral ministry. She had labored 17 years in Peru, 10 in Bolivia, but was increasingly frustrated by regulations that, she believed, impeded her work. She had heard about the ministry of Blessed Charles de Foucauld while working in Peru. In 1989 her sister sent her a copy of The Extension magazine in which she read about a nun in Maryland who had founded an order modeled on Brother Charles's rule. "I had been inspired by his willingness to let God be the guide of his daily life, of his utter abandonment to the will of God. Reading about Sr. Mary Elizabeth, I thought, here was a kindred spirit. Sister, like Charles, wanted to 'cry the gospel with her life.' And there was something dynamic about her order, something quite the opposite of the rigidity that inhibited me, a freedom to work among and for the poor."

Sr. Mary Joseph wanted to join the Little Sisters of Jesus and Mary, but leaving the Peruvian community and their mission was such a painful ordeal—"like a divorce," she said sadly. "I dearly loved the founders and sisters who had been such a blessing in my life for 26 years. When I left, I left part of my heart behind there. It's still there." She wanted a simpler life; she wanted to be part of a community faithful to Church teachings, to wear a habit, to pray and live together with her community—and continue to minister to the abandoned parishes in the Andes. Would such a ministry be possible for her as a Little Sister? 'Come for a visit,' Sr. Mary Elizabeth said. 'We'll talk. We'll see if that will work.'

"So I came to Salisbury. I instantly felt embraced by Sister's openness of spirit and her warmth. She was so genuine and so humble. My fondest memories of that visit were of sitting on the floor with Sister playing with the dogs. Sister adored those dogs. I love dogs, too. My dog saved me from loneliness when my mother got sick. I was just a forlorn little girl, and my dog, Bunny Jane, seemed to understand how I was suffering, how lonely for my mother I was. Ziggy and Fresca—those were Sr. Mary Elizabeth's dogs at that time. They were just mutts, like my Bunny Jane. To be polite I asked Sister what kind of dogs they were. 'Well, they don't have any pedigree,' she said. 'They're just like us; there's nothing pedigree about any of us here.'"

But, Sr. Mary Joseph says, Sr. Mary Elizabeth was charismatic. "Tourists would wander into the book store we ran in Ocean City, and before they left, if Sister Mary Elizabeth happened to be there, they'd be volunteering some of their precious vacation time.

Her attitude was, she was giving them a chance to do God's work, and that was really the greatest gift of all." Sr. Mary Joseph pauses, looks away, as if seeing Sister again as she was those many years ago. Quietly, smiling, she says, "She was so much fun to be with. I called her a go-go girl. Even when she was so impaired, needing oxygen to breathe and a cane to walk, she was indomitable. I was often with her on her visits to destitute families in the country. One day as I was hesitating to make a turn in traffic, Sister declared with authority and without hesitation, 'When you're going to do something BAD, do it fast!' I think she knew this would be the one thing she taught me that I'd never forget!"

One summer early in Sr. Mary Joseph's training, she and Sr. Mary Elizabeth took a break from their book store labors to enjoy a picnic on the beach. "After searching in vain for a parking place, Sister noticed a family headed for their car. 'Look! They're leaving!' They pulled out; we slid into the vacated spot. As we walked toward the beach, Sister threw her arms up and exclaimed, 'Thank you, Jesus!' When we returned to the car there was a parking ticket on the windshield. We had parked in a No Parking space. Back at the shop, Sister Mary Elizabeth walked past a picture of a smiling Christ we called "The Laughing Jesus." 'You were laughing at me when I thanked you, knowing I'd get a ticket,' she fondly reproached Him. Jesus was real for her. Real in His gifts, whether buildings or awards, illnesses and difficulties, phone calls, meetings, poor and homeless people, even hungry dogs abandoned in back yards to whom she would have the sisters bring water day after day."

"I was also with Sister when she traveled to Chicago to receive the Lumen Christi award from the Extension Society to be presented by Cardinal Bernardin. An hour before the ceremony, attended by hundreds of distinguished guests, I went to find her, expecting that she would be working on her acceptance remarks which she hadn't had time to compose, hoping she wasn't too overwhelmed by the prospect of this event. Rather than being anxiously at work, when I entered her room she was sitting in front of the television watching "Mister Rogers' Neighborhood." I guess if anyone could

Sister Mary Elizabeth receives the Lumen Christi award from Cardinal Joseph Bernardin, Chicago, 1989. Attending, at left, Father Edward Slattery, President, Catholic Extension, and the Most Reverend Robert Mulvee, Bishop of Wilmington.

calm one's nerves it was kindly Mister Rogers, but I think Sister could have taught him one or two things about serenity of spirit. She had such trust in God, trust that He would inspire her words, that all would be well. And it was.

"In spite of her 89 years, chronic cough, her oxygen tank, her foot ailments, her digestive problems, her heart attack and strokes, her arthritis and poor circulation, Sr. Mary Elizabeth was up and about, going to meetings, visiting the needy, making stops at the hospital and at nursing homes. She was always—always!—available. And every day she traveled back and forth from Princess Anne to Salisbury, one-half hour each way, rarely missing Mass, the prayers and activities of the community, or her precious hour of private meditation and adoration.

"One summer Sr. Marilyn's family invited Sr. Mary Elizabeth to visit them at their summer cottage in Wisconsin. She could hardly move, but she wanted to go, despite the two-day trip in the blazing hot weather, despite the bulky oxygen machine that accompanied her now wherever she went, despite the dreadful trucks hurling around the beltways of Chicago and Minneapolis. She did it! She went! And she went out on the pontoon boat ride, too. She was definitely our go-go girl! And she wanted all of us to live that way, to live life to the full. Each of the sisters, once professed, was to go on a pilgrimage to the Holy Land, and we were all to make occasional trips to the Shrine of St. Joseph in Montreal.

"Sr. Mary Elizabeth made friends easily—she had so many good friends! Of course, not everybody felt the same about her. Our bishop back then was frustrated by her independence. He told her she was the kind of woman who didn't worry about asking permission, and he was right. And she was very outspoken, too. She had confrontations with the mayor, and with one of our state's senators, and with corporate big shots. She treated everyone the same, and some didn't like that."

It didn't take Sr. Mary Joseph long to relinquish her dream of being a Little Sister of Jesus and Mary in Peru. Within a month of her visit, while Sr. Connie, Sr.Patricia and Sr. Mary Elizabeth were attending to the needs of the poor at the Crisis Center, Sr. Mary Joseph found herself supervising the daily operations of the book shop. "Sister just gave it to me to run," she recalled. "I don't know how she knew I'd be good at it, but I was pretty good at it."

She never returned to Peru. Sr. Mary Elizabeth had too many projects underway or in the planning stages on the Eastern Shore to spare anyone for a foreign mission anywhere.

Mary Ann Ware wore the denim of the Little Sisters of Jesus and Mary from 1984 till 1998. She was 26 years old when she joined the order. "I was so cocky. I thought I knew all about life. I had gone to college in the 70's until my money ran out. And my interest ran out, too." After that she worked at several jobs on the Eastern Shore. "This was and is my home. I grew up knowing about Sr. Mary Elizabeth and the nuns. My mother had been an almost full-time volunteer with them while I was growing up, and my dad volunteered, too. The nuns were like extended family."

In between jobs at one point in 1982, she decided to go with her mother to the convent. "Sr. Mary Elizabeth knew I was coming over to help out, and she came out onto the convent's porch to greet me. I could feel immediately that she was just this loving and humble woman. And she had this playful twinkle in her eyes. I thought, 'This is going to be fun!' I was so impressed by her. She literally radiated goodness. When I got to know her better, she would tell me stories about her years with the Little Sisters of the Poor. In one of the hospitals where she worked, one of her jobs was to wash, dry, fold and shelve the bedding. 'The Mother Superior was so strict with us,' she told me. 'One day after I had shelved a day's worth of laundry, she came into the closet and knocked all the sheets and pillow cases onto the floor.' Why, I asked her, shocked by the seeming cruelty of the act. 'I think she was trying to teach me humility and obedience. We were expected to be super human.' But, she concluded, her training there made her strong as steel—and nothing was able to dim the twinkle or diminish the humor, the gentleness, the hospitality."

"Sister was such a healer. And a teacher! She taught classes on faith formation and theology, she sent us to workshops on poverty and religion, we went on so many retreats and learned from the Jesuits and from the monks at Berryville. Just an

awesome education. She was deeply knowledge-
able, but her wisdom was most effectively revealed
in how she lived her faith. Honestly, I was in awe of
her learning. She could be pretty dogmatic, pretty
domineering. She once told us that there were lots
of books that we didn't need to read, that there were
only five books worth knowing! Imagine, being so
sure of such a thing!"

It might have been that certitude, in part, that
was responsible for the ministry losing many of its
best volunteers during the 1990's. "One of our most
skilled lay volunteers resigned one day, and Sr. Mary
Elizabeth was devastated and didn't know why it
happened. But I knew. The volunteer had voiced
many valid complaints and concerns and criticisms
about the operations of the Crisis Center, but Sister
couldn't seem to hear other views. So we lost this
treasure whom everybody loved. Sr. Mary Elizabeth
couldn't hear her. She had her way of doing things
and just knew she was right."

"We also had difficulties attracting and retain-
ing women for the order. Sr. Mary Elizabeth had
been profoundly influenced by the writings of Jean
Vanier, the founder of L'Arche," an international
federation dedicated to the creation and growth of
homes, programs, and support networks for people
who have intellectual disabilities." According to
Mary Ann, Sister wanted to welcome such women
into the order, but increasingly they proved to be
more difficult to work with than she had expected. "Soon after I joined the order, Sister asked me
to work in Baltimore where she had reopened a

mission operation after several years' absence. Sr. Connie and I sort of headed up the mission, and one of the women Sr. Mary Elizabeth sent with us had, we discovered, multiple personality disorder. She went to counseling for her problem, but it didn't help and her behavior made it more and more difficult for us to do the work. Finally, Sr. Mary Elizabeth had to let her go, but it was a terrible blow to her heart, it was just terribly hard on her."

"Another candidate for the order, during a class at the convent one day, made a claim about her identity that made us all realize how truly sick she was, and that she needed to be hospitalized. Again, Sr. Mary Elizabeth was devastated, not because she was losing a member, but because she was losing a soul. She held these wounded people to her heart, wanted to help them, and was haunted by her inability to heal them. They were all wonderful people," Mary Ann said about several women who had to be sent away. "You felt you were on holy ground when you were with them. It reminded you of the strength of the human spirit, to witness what people can endure. All of these women were difficult to live and work with, but they all gave something to the convent, even if it was only their brokenness."

Mary Ann left the order in 1998. "I fell in love," she said simply. But, she insisted, the 14 years she spent as a Little Sister of Jesus and Mary were the best years of her life. "As soon as you start working with the poor, you encounter your own ignorance. Where have I been all my life? What fantasy world have I been living in?" The Baltimore years exhaust-

Sr. Mary Elizabeth, lower right, with the Little Sisters of Jesus and Mary, 1995

ed her and she had to return to Salisbury, but, she said, "I wouldn't exchange that time of trial for anything because every struggle was so rich. Really, it was like a great gift. Leaving was the hardest thing I've ever done in my life. I've been away from the order now for as many years as I spent in it, and I still think back on that time with tremendous gratitude. And when I think back, I always see that bright, smiling face of Sr. Mary Elizabeth."

Fr. John Abrahams slouches comfortably in the sitting room off the main entrance of the Little Sisters of Jesus and Mary convent in Salisbury. He wraps himself against the chill in the room in a threadbare Nike blue and grey "hoodie," inspired, he laughs, by Sr. Mary Elizabeth's fashion example. He met her in 1975. "I was doing my novitiate at St. Peter the Apostle Church in Baltimore. My pastoral supervisor was pastor there—John Delclos—and he was great friends with Sr. Mary Elizabeth." Father Abrahams first met her at the Joseph House gift store in an area of the city that is now a dangerous slum. He was intrigued and impressed by the uniqueness and diversity of the goods Joseph House had for sale, and it quickly became clear to him that Sr. Mary Elizabeth was the principal buyer. "Before Pier 1, before 10,000 Villages, Sr. Mary Elizabeth was importing hand-crafted items from Africa and the Far East," he marvels.

He had never seen a nun in that kind of setting,

working behind the counter in a shop, clothed in rough denim. He remembers his first impression, of a restrained, quiet respectful woman who radiated such sincere hospitality—a consequence, he believed, of her devotion to Brother Charles. "Her faith was straightforward, unadorned. Her prayers seemed to be given to her by God, and her ministry was, too. She had no doubts about that at all. She was genuinely, sincerely, purely doing what she was supposed to do." He pauses, and looks disbelievingly. "That certitude: it's sort of loony!"

At the store, John Abrahams and Fr. Delclos joined Sr. Mary Elizabeth for prayer in a tiny chapel off the main room of the shop. There were no chairs, no benches, only kneelers, he recalls. On the way home, Fr. Delclos commented that there were those in the diocese who thought Sr. Mary Elizabeth and Sr. Patricia were "goofy," a judgment that might have revealed, he speculated, on just how far the traditional Church had drifted from the teachings of Christ. "The poet Theodore Roethke wrote that 'God has to be bored with organized religion.' Jesus' quarrel with the Pharisees is replicated over and over, and this is yet another example of it. It's always the same: the structure, the hierarchy gets in the way of the ministry. Sr. Mary Elizabeth broke through the barriers that kept so many from doing Jesus' work, but she never broke away."

He spent his days studying at St. Mary's Seminary, but he needed the hospitality, the welcoming warmth that Sr. Mary Elizabeth offered him, and often he would spend weekends working and living at Joseph House. He recalled with special affection the chapel on Eutaw Place. Here he learned from Sr. Mary Elizabeth about Brother Charles de Foucault who lived the monk's charism and who instilled this young seminarian with his spirit. "She lived in the midst of those she served, foregoing the comforts of traditional convent life which often afforded ministers an escape and haven. For Sr. Mary Elizabeth there was no escape. She received her comfort from the poor."

Fr. Abrahams found in the Little Sisters of Jesus and Mary what he searched for and couldn't find in the Church of that time. Sr. Mary Elizabeth, he felt, emanated a spirit of grace that was still alive in the Church but was hard to find. She had tapped into the buried roots of the Church that were concealed from many in the mainstream Church. She had a pre-Vatican view of the Church, but she was grateful for the freedom the Council afforded her to establish her unique ministry. "She reprehended license. She was an orthodox rebel, never moving ahead without approval from the bishop where she felt his approval was required."

He recalled that at her funeral, Bishop Salterelli, citing Sr. Mary Elizabeth's many admirable deeds, confessed that she accomplished many of them despite his supervision. She did wonderful things without letting the bishop know about them. "She was painstakingly obedient, but was also a free spirit. She could always find wiggle room amidst the regulations and the rules to go where she wanted to go."

"She was a go-getter, very down-to-earth, and beneath her hardworking pragmatism she experienced a deep intimacy with God. She had found in Brother Charles a way of serving God that she had searched for for so long. His influence on her was incalculable, especially his insistence on his littleness. She shared that humility, never wanting to be at the head of the table. She identified through Charles's teaching with Jesus of Nazareth, with the hidden life of Jesus, before his public ministry. Charles eschewed the public life, and Sister Elizabeth was also drawn to that life of quietude. Charles writes about wanting to be able to die, scattered over the ground, crucified, dying in pure love. Sister Teresa of Lisieux died that way. They had no concern about their lives; they offered them up as Christ offered his. Sr. Mary Elizabeth shared this mystical spirit with these saints, this willingness to be ground to death by God."

"She was always very gentle to me," Father Abrahams says quietly. "She loved broken people, and I am one of those. I feel that with her and because of her I have shared the truth of my Christian faith. Her love was so utterly authentic, you just felt it to be coming from God. I experienced her presence and love in an intimate and personal way, and I sense them even now, and know that I will be comforted by them in an even deeper way in Heaven. Her love never ends; it is there for me, for all of us, forever."

Dan McDonald lives across from Joseph House convent in Nazareth House with three other permanent volunteers. He first met Sr. Mary Elizabeth in 1990. He had completed his Master's degree in Marine Studies at the University of Delaware and was unsure of his life's direction. In graduate school he had begun to study scripture and knew without a doubt that he wanted to live the gospel, not just study it. Dan knew that James was speaking to him when he urged those gathered to hear him to be "doers of the word and not hearers only, deluding yourselves." (James I, 22) And the doers, in his estimation, were those for whom all of suffering humanity were brothers and sisters.

Much of his graduate work had been done in Lewes, Delaware, and there he had heard of these nuns and their mission in nearby Salisbury, Maryland. He drove to Salisbury to meet with Sr. Mary Elizabeth soon after graduating, and made up his mind to live and work with the Little Sisters of Jesus and Mary. He was amazed by the utter devotion of the sisters to helping the poor. He had not known such people or organizations existed, and he knew he wanted to be a part of it.

"Sister reminded me of my grandmother. The way she spoke—very soft, very gentle. So welcoming. She was just such a soothing, tender, warm-hearted presence. The sisters had installed a chapel on the first floor off the main entrance of the convent. She invited me to enter with her. I was shocked to see an old dog stretched in sleep across the front of the tabernacle. 'That's Ziggy, our watchdog,' Sister said playfully, 'but he doesn't watch much.' " The chapel was a refuge from the endless crises the nuns confronted each day, but there was never enough time for prayerful contemplation. Dan had experienced great stretches of solitude and meditation while studying at Lewes, and he was searching for a life which would balance action for Christ's sake with contemplation of Him. The sisters could never seem to find that balance. "They couldn't set boundaries for themselves," he said. "Sr. Mary Elizabeth tried to provide time—retreats at Berryville and in Pennsylvania, the novitiate at Princess Anne. But they were always overwhelmed, all of them. I was so moved by their devotion, and the realization that Sr. Mary Elizabeth was the inspiration for it. But I also knew that they had to keep searching for that balance between prayer and work, or they would destroy themselves."

Dan left after two years, still searching for his own way to best serve God. He joined the Oblates of Mary Immaculate, but just before taking final vows, after six years of study and missionary work, he knew that God was not calling him to the Oblate way of life. He had kept in touch with Sr. Mary Elizabeth throughout those six years, and when he told her he was leaving the seminary, she invited him to return to Salisbury to live and work at Joseph House. What he had been looking for finally found him. He has been with the sisters ever since. "I would do anything that needed doing," Dan says. "I worked at the Crisis Center, directing clients to counselors and controlling the crowds that sometimes threatened to overwhelm the place. I'd do yard work in Salisbury and Princess Anne, at the cloister there. And I'd do home visitations with Sr. Mary Elizabeth. They were so important to Sister, to see the conditions under which these families struggled, to witness how they cared for their children—things you can't learn in an interview. For such a gentle person, Sister was often angry--with landlords for exorbitant rents for slum-like housing, with the poultry industry because they worked their employees so hard for so little and gave them no job security at all. You could see the suffering and sadness and anger all flashing from her face."

When Dan left for the Oblates, the Crisis Center had over 5000 active files, and the Joseph House Village (now the Village of Hope) had just opened. When he returned in 1998, that number had not diminished. The sisters had opened Nazareth House, a residence adjacent to the convent for permanent volunteers. They had established the Joseph House cloister in Princess Anne, and Mountaire Farms had donated the building next to the Crisis Center that would eventually become Joseph House Workshop, a residence facility for men. "Sister would tell us what she was thinking of doing. We'd be skeptical, and exhausted by the work we were doing already. But she would move ahead—with the Cloister, the Village, the Workshop—and they would come into being, and there were always people willing to help."

Dan taught classes for the sisters on issues of poverty and justice, and introductory classes on pastoral care. He also began to organize the archives and edit the newsletter while continuing to help at the Center and accompanying Sr. Mary Elizabeth on her home visits. Then one day in 2001, as he was helping Sister into the car at the convent, she said she needed someone to work in the gift shop in Ocean City and asked him, very casually, if that was something he'd be interested in doing. "She wanted me to manage, but she wouldn't say so. That was her method! And she always got what she wanted." The store wasn't making any money for Joseph House, but it gave the Little Sisters a presence in the vacation community, and it attracted volunteers and contributions without which the ministry simply could not function. "We had a chapel in the store, too, and many vacationers were grateful for a quiet place to pray in the midst of the happy tumult of the beach. Sister loved going to fairs—in Chicago, New York City, Montreal—to find beautiful and inspiring products for sale in the store. And she had an incredibly discerning eye. Truly, she could do anything and everything."

Dan says he feels even closer to Sr. Mary Elizabeth since her death. He spends most of his time now in the archives researching Sister and the Little Sisters, so it's as if they're in constant communication. "She is always in my thoughts. I saw little of her in the last years of her life. She was very frail and spent much of her time at the Novitiate in Princess Anne while I was almost entirely preoccupied with running the store at the beach for 10 years, from 2001 until it was closed in 2011. I visited her in Princess Anne shortly before she died with a friend, an Oblate who, it so happened, had travelled with Sister to Lourdes in 1991 and had come to the Shore to meet with her once more. He hadn't known that she was in such bad health. Then I saw her, for the last time, at the store. It was the Friday before she died. A friend had driven her down. She came in, looked around, and bought a book. I was writing up the sales ticket, and I looked up to see her, cane on one side and oxygen tank on the other, her little body bent forward, slowly stepping into the warm sun of the day. That was the last I saw her alive. I have always wished that I would have known it. There is so much I have wanted to talk with her about."

Maria Gitin first met Sr. Mary Elizabeth in 1994 after moving to Salisbury. She remembered seeing her coming into church and thinking, before ever meeting her, that she had a strength and vibrancy and that she must be someone very special. A new friend who belonged to a group of women at church, the Mary Martha Guild, that prepared lunches for the Crisis Center, invited her to help one day and she loved the place and the work. She told Sr. Patricia that she wanted to volunteer. Sr. Patricia introduced her to Sr. Carolyn, who introduced her to two men, two brand new volunteers like herself. "She said to us, 'This is what we need, this is what you need to do. The people who were supposed to do it didn't show up. Okay, I've got to go.' The three of us looked at each other and realized we needed to put a meal together for these hungry people. And we did, and we got pretty good at it, and even recruited more volunteers to help us. It was during this time that I got to know Sr. Mary Elizabeth. Every now and then she would come into the kitchen to say hello and ask what we were doing. Well, the energy that emanated from her was so incredible. It was infectious. I remember thinking, 'what more can I do?' after working all day in the Center. She had this strength of personality, this incredible energy that drew you to her and brought out of you the best you had to give to someone else. She had the power to draw people to her to do the work she needed to get done and couldn't do alone."

Maria said that Sr. Mary Elizabeth was "unstoppable," and that she had a remarkable humility which allowed her to begin a project, but then give it to others to continue and complete, having no need to reap the praise or gratitude for the work being done. She was also astute and sensible and shrewd in her dealings with everyone, clients and volunteers alike. "In the early years, when she was working at the Crisis Center, she'd witness people driving into the lot in large SUV's, and she'd ask them very directly, 'What are you doing here? Why do you need our food if you can afford a car like that?' " She was, Maria said, an amazing blend of compassion and common sense. She knew there would always be people taking a free lunch or money for an electric bill who didn't need it, who'd then use the money ordinarily spent on those things for something less healthful, such as drink or drugs. But she also knew that if she helped ten people who truly needed help out of twenty who got help, the Center was doing God's work. "She taught us that our discretion had to be leavened with compassion, or it could be a harmful thing. We had to learn that we were doing God's work, not our own. She once said, 'Why, it's so simple, the work we do. If a man comes in and tells you he has no job and hasn't eaten in two days, you don't do an in-depth analysis of his socio-economic deficiencies. You give him a bag of groceries and a dollar if you have it. If you don't have a dollar, you keep asking people you know until someone gives it to you.'"

Years Of Growth:
The Crisis Center

Today, Dave Heininger directs the Crisis Center from a cramped little office in a converted trailer fronting the center. He sits hunched over a messy desk nursing crippling back pain that will require considerable surgery. He shuffles paper and, despite the center's being closed this day, listens to each recorded call from people needing help and explains that he'll call them back later in the day. He winces a bit, but he smiles more. He's tall and somewhat imposing, but his voice and eyes are gentle. He must be approaching 70, but he seems much younger.

He has lived in Nazareth House, the permanent volunteer residence for men across the street from the convent, for 17 years. Following a stint in the Army, he moved to California, graduated from college, worked for a bank, then became a partner in a small printing company. " I was pretty active in my church out there, and had always dreamed of being a priest. In 1995, I made the biggest decision of my life; I sold my house and car, resigned from the printing company, gave my cats away, and got on a plane bound for Milwaukee to join the priests of the Sacred Heart community. "

After a year in formation and six months in his novitiate in Chicago, Dave decided he could not accept the restrictive regulations of that life. "I went back to L.A., feeling lost. I talked to a vocations director out there and he advised me to find a ministry where I could devote myself for a year and contemplate God's will for my life. I checked out the vocations book—there are hundreds of places you can go if you're interested!" At about this time he read the Extension magazine article about Sr. Mary Elizabeth receiving the Lumen Christi award. After several phone conversations with Sr. Pat Lennon and Sr. Connie, my mind was made up. I bought a car, drove across the country to Maryland and knocked on the door of the convent. Once that door opened, my life changed forever. I had found what God wanted me to do. After 17 years I'm still here, working with the sisters, working for the poor."

The day after he knocked on the door, this former business executive was washing blinds and mopping floors. "Soon I was doing all sorts of jobs they needed me to do. I interviewed clients at the Crisis Center during the mornings and visited families out in the country in the afternoon. On weekends I worked at the bookstore, and I'd also go down to cut the grass at the novitiate in Princess Anne. Sr. Mary Elizabeth was living there and one day she called me in for a 'little talk'. It didn't take me long to figure out what she wanted without quite saying so. I finally asked her, 'Sister, are you trying to tell me that you want me to be the director of the Crisis Center?' She said, 'Yes, David, that's what I want.' I've been doing it ever since."

When it opened in 1984, the Crisis Center was confined to one large one-story cinderblock warehouse building and a trailer. In a 1987 interview with Extension Magazine's Father Patrick Brankin, Sr. Mary Elizabeth reflected on the challenges the sisters faced (and still face today) attempting to give aid to the poor. " 'Some days we have much, and many days we have little. . . .I tell the sisters, much is better, but—much or little—we always have God!' "

Father Brankin offered this portrait of the Center three years after it opened: "The scene at Joseph House is one of organized mayhem. In the dining room, several dozen people are eating a free lunch prepared by members of a neighborhood church and served under the direction of the Little Sisters. In the back, families wait patiently for bags of groceries. In a renovated trailer that sits beside Joseph House another family looks for children's coats and shoes among the neatly labeled boxes of donated clothing.

"Everywhere the gentle touch of the sisters is evident. Sr. Teresita handles incoming calls at the front desk. Sr. Theresa keeps a sharp eye on the length of the lines. Sr. Patricia speaks quietly with a young mother. Sr. Mary Elizabeth looks at her sisters affectionately.

" 'Can you feel the peace here?' she asks. 'That peace comes from the sisters themselves. We take women into our community just as they are. They don't have to be perfect, they only have to love. Each sister has the capacity to do something special for God. We help them develop those capacities, but we never hide our faults. We know we are all broken people healing other broken people through God's love.[2] There's no make-believe in our life. That in itself brings us peace.' "

The Center has expanded significantly since it opened in 1984 when it was confined to that one cinderblock building and a trailer. Today groceries are distributed each month to over 1900 families. There are 5000 active files each representing families with children, single mothers, unemployed fathers, the aged and infirm. The food is donated mainly by local restaurants, grocery stores and government agencies; and individuals donate upwards of a third of the food given out three days each week. In addition, thirteen local churches take turns providing hot meals that they prepare in the center's large kitchen for approximately 130 people 3 days each week. There's also a shower and a laundry, and soap, towels, toothpaste and deodorant for about 30 homeless men and women, and a hospitality room where they can watch television, socialize and stay warm on cold days. They enjoy breakfast and lunch five days a week.

On its two-acre industrial lot the Center also contains an enormous warehouse which serves as a storage area for food, clothing and other

2   Brankin, Fr. Patrick. "A New Community Grows." Extension August/September, 1987:12-15.

donated materials. A large truck ferries supplies from storage to a loading dock at the center, past two enormous walk-in freezers. "We used to have a furniture ministry, too," Dave says, as he walks across the gravel yard to the warehouse, "but we had to close it up. The beds we got often had bugs, and other things donated were broken. Then we found out people were selling what we gave them. It's too bad, but we can't operate like that." Back in his office, Dave talks about his devotion to Sr. Mary Elizabeth and the work she pioneered. "She was driven to help everyone, anyone who was suffering from poverty and neglect. Nothing would keep her from doing what she could to alleviate the anguish and misery she found all around her. She hauled that damn oxygen tank around with her for the last three years of her life and never broke her stride. 99 percent of our clients had no connection to our Church, but that didn't matter to Sister. I honestly believe that Heaven for her is a place where she can give comfort to others eternally. She never praised our work; she thought we were rewarded by having an opportunity to help those who came seeking our help. If you didn't commit 100 percent of your effort to your work, you didn't last long. She was the guiding light, and there won't be anyone like her again."

The stories of those in need seeking help at Joseph House are depressingly repetitive and

Sister Mary Elizabeth and Hattie Phillips, a devoted employee at the Crisis Center.

yet those stories' conclusions are almost always inspiring, moving testaments to the bonds of love forged by Sr. Mary Elizabeth's vision. Every Tuesday, Wednesday and Thursday, long lines of destitute and downtrodden men, women and children queue up before the Crisis Center interview vestibule and the food trailer. Patiently they shuffle forward, trusting that the volunteers and the sisters will help them with the commonplace crises that assail the poor and that are anything but trivial to them.

Angel, 27, the mother of two young children, had been abandoned by her husband who informed her that he was going to get a divorce. Angel recently had surgery for carpal tunnel syndrome and had been unable to work for several weeks. With no financial support from her husband, she quickly fell behind making payments on her bills. She had applied for food stamps and assistance from the Department of Social Services for rent, but they were unable to help her with her electricity bill. Joseph House paid $200 to have the electricity turned back on in Angel's home. She was profoundly grateful for the assistance, but as she departed she worried about losing her car insurance before she could go back to work.

Gary, a 57 year old disabled veteran, was weak from chemotherapy treatments he was receiving for his cancer; he was unable to work and was struggling to pay his bills. The volunteer who interviewed Gary recommended that the Center pay a $250 gas bill, and also made sure that Gary left that day with an ample allotment of food, especially fresh fruits and vegetables. Another volunteer went to visit Gary at his home and helped him switch to a less expensive phone company, and also contacted a representative from the Veteran's Administration who made arrangement to visit Gary to make sure he was receiving the help that he had earned serving his country.

Nancy, 73, was crying when she called Joseph House in late January. She was confined to a wheelchair, was living on a fixed income, and had no heat or light in her home because she had been unable to pay a $530 electric bill. She was frightened and cold. The electric company would not reduce Nancy's bill, and would not restore her power until the following day. The director of the Crisis Center told the representative of the electric company that that was simply not acceptable. Following a lengthy and heated discussion with the company supervisor, the Crisis Center interviewer had Nancy's heat restored later that day. Nancy now works with a volunteer counselor who is helping her budget her limited income.

There are thousands of such stories in the Center's records of its work over the past 28 years. Each brings together a person or family snared in a quandary or confronted with an emergency, and a sympathetic new friend who is happy to be able to offer assistance and acceptance and kindness of heart.

The Village

Sr. Mary Elizabeth's desire to help people solve the root of their problems never left her. She witnessed first-hand the generational spread of poverty as a way of life that was passed on from parent to child. Many people helped through Joseph House had never experienced the supportive family environment that would enable them to become self-sufficient adults. Sr. Mary Elizabeth remembered the small but important triumphs achieved with the Montessori School in Baltimore and she prayed that God would show the way toward bringing the same type of rehabilitation to broken families on the Eastern Shore. She wanted to give people the same supportive and stable environments that would allow them to discover themselves, their abilities, and their intrinsic worth as children of God.

One answer to her prayers came in 1987 when developers Bob and Debbie Miller consulted her for ideas regarding low-income housing projects for the poor. The Millers had been for some time staunch supporters of both Joseph House and Habitat for Humanity. From their discussions with Sr. Mary Elizabeth arose the idea of a housing village where the displaced poor could live while receiving education, counseling and emotional support for themselves and their children. In June, 1988, the Millers formed a non-profit organization, Caritas, Inc., to develop Joseph House Village.

A five-acre site was purchased on a rise above Johnson Pond in Salisbury, state grants were applied for, and local fundraising began in earnest. Sr. Mary Elizabeth was appointed to the board of directors and strove to keep the vision and purpose of the project in focus, imbuing the development of the village with a spirit of selfless giving and faith in God's providence.

After three years of planning and preparation, construction of Building I of what was envisioned as a six-building project began March, 19, 1991, the feast of St. Joseph. Opened in October, 1991, the Village was another step in Sr. Mary Elizabeth's faith pilgrimage. From the singular effort she originated from the basement in Baltimore in 1965, her struggles to help the poor had increased a thousand-fold and more with the help of more sisters, volunteers and donors.

Today the village consists of two buildings, one a residence for fourteen families, the second containing classrooms for workshops on parenting, financial planning and job skills, meeting rooms, a playroom for the children, and offices for the administrators who oversee the operation of the village—a director, administrative assistant, a director of tutoring services, a case worker who counsels, directs and advises the families, ensuring that they're making progress toward their goals of self-sufficiency and responsible citizenship.

Since its opening in 1991, over 600 women, many with children, have lived in the residence wing. Some leave on their own soon after they arrive, deciding that they're not suited to living in a program with what they feel are unacceptable restrictions on their lives–on who can and cannot stay in the residence, for example. Others are asked to leave because they don't pay their rent (30% of their monthly income) or don't take care of their rooms or don't make educational or vocational progress or don't abide by the rules about drinking, drugs or visitations. Those who stay for the program are allowed two years of residence, and many ask for and receive extensions on that limit.

The women of the re-named Village of Hope have all experienced crises in their lives that have compelled them to apply for residency. Many are single parents who have lost their jobs, or have endured domestic abuse, or have been addicts—or, in many cases, all of these things. All of them are homeless when they come to the Village, and most have one, two or three young children who are in desperate need of the security a home and a regimen bestows. According to Jasmine Rogers, the Village of Hope's case worker, roughly 80% of these women suffer from some form of psychological illness ranging from bi-polar disorder to severe depression. Their needs are extensive and pervasive, and the Village of Hope offers them every opportunity to seek the healing they need. All of them appear to come to the Village suffering from feelings of failure and low self-esteem.

At the Village, they are required to take classes to improve their education and job prospects. More importantly, they're obliged to attend workshops that teach basic life skills—parenting, personal finances, nutrition, child health care. Both individual and group psychological counseling sessions are also mandatory and crucial elements of the program. Here women work mainly on developing interpersonal skills and on repairing their damaged self-esteem. These counseling services are also available for the children, many of whom are in need of the attention and direction, and there is a mandatory after-school tutoring program for the children as well.

"We try to teach them that they can break the damaging cycle that they have lived in for most of their lives," says Ms. Rogers. "They meet with me at least once each week. I make sure they're succeeding with their coursework, and I will help them make contacts with people in the community who can help them get work or further counseling. I also work to resolve any conflicts between residents, and make sure the residents know what they are expected to do and not do in the Village. I want them to know that I'm always there for them, even if they have issues. I want to provide them with an island of calm in the midst of their emotional storms."

The climax of Aleia's story may not typify the stories of many other women who have lived at the Village, but her life that led to the Village is all too representative. In an interview with the diocesan newspaper, Aleia told of the insanity of her life before undergoing recovery and moving to the Village. She was often drunk or strung out on drugs, she said, for twelve years living a defiant, wayward, undisciplined existence that jeopardized the welfare of her three children who would eventually be taken away from her and placed in foster care. She and her husband both were substance abusers, she said, but she would not admit it, even to herself.

Then, in 1993, she said she had an insight into how she was squandering her life and ruining the lives of three innocent children. She sought help, went through a rehabilitation program, attended AA, and lived in a halfway house as she strove to be reunited with her children. Then she heard about the Village of Hope (then known as Joseph House Village). She was accepted after being interviewed several times by the selection committee. "I was ready for regulations," she said in an interview in 1997. "I wasn't ready to be living on my own. I needed people I could lean on. I wanted change. I was sick of the insanity. I needed this place."

Aleia is certain that what she learned from the classes and counseling at the Village enabled her to take responsibility for herself and for her children. She got a salaried position with Americorps, which pleased her because it gave her the opportunity to do the kind of work she loves—helping other people. At the same time, she studied for a degree in accounting, volunteered at the Village, and raised five children (her three and two who came into her life with her new husband). "This program works for those who want it," Aleia told a correspondent for The Dialog, the diocesan paper. "It works for those who really want to change their lives and make something of themselves and not live in the insanity they were living in that brought them to the Village in the first place."

Miriam and her two children came to Joseph House Village in 1993. Her husband was chemically dependent on drugs, could not be depended on to help with the children, and was frequently absent from their home. Miriam became worried about the children and realized that their lives would only get worse if she stayed in the marriage and didn't make some serious changes in her life. This realization led her to Joseph House Village. Miriam decided, on her first day at the Village, that she was going to follow the rules and make the best of the situation. She understood that this opportunity was a great blessing.

Soon after her arrival, she enrolled in classes at a local community college in order to be more employable. She followed the Village rules, and readily assumed responsibility for work that needed doing in the Village. Indeed, she was heavily relied upon to drive the Village van to transport other residents to school or to their jobs. She was conscientious about paying her rent, and took pride in telling her sponsor how she was paying off other bills that she and her husband had accumulated.

Today, Cathy is in the throes of leaving the Village after spending two years living, learning and working toward her goal of being an independent, responsible mother for her three sons. Her story, despite the singularity of its details, traces a common arc with which many of the inhabitants, past and present, could identify.

As a child, Cathy lived part of the year in Salisbury, part in Baltimore City with her grandparents. In Salisbury she lived with her father and his girlfriend, who didn't like Cathy at all. "The state had decided that my mother's mental illness made her incapable of caring for me, so I ended up with my father who wasn't very good at child-rearing. And I wasn't the easiest kid to get along with. I was angry at my father for not protecting me from his girlfriend. I became rebellious, dropped out of middle school before I was 15, never attended high school. I was partying, doing drugs and alcohol when I was 14."

When the girlfriend's son moved in with them, there wasn't room for them all. "So the girlfriend decided I had to go," Cathy says with a bitterness that has moderated only slightly over the past 15 years, "and my father went along with it. Basically,

I've been on my own since I was 14."

Cathy has been in The Village of Hope for a little over 2 years. In the first two months she attended psychological counseling and parenting meetings. Then she began GED classes and qualified for her Certified Nursing Assistant certificate. She now works as a Certified Nursing Assistant (Geriatrics) and she says this is a big accomplishment for her. Very soon she and the boys will move into a home that is subsidized in part by the Tri-County Alliance for the Homeless. She is both thrilled and anxious, but she knows that she will prevail over the dark forces that nearly destroyed her because she has learned at the Village how to be a responsible parent and citizen.

The Village has been an absolute blessing, she says, though frustrating at times: "It was hard for me to have curfews and to be told who could and who could not visit me in my apartment." But she struggled to follow the rules for her children's sake. The Village of Hope provided her with a home for her kids, and it gave the kids stability and structure, a safe and lovely place to play and study, a place of love and tutoring and advising. Now, she says, she's having a hard time leaving. "The kids have had this huge yard with bike trails and friends and woods and so much space. It's going to be hard to leave this place, and hard to leave some of the people I've become friends with. I've gotten my education here, and my certification. The Village made sure I had transportation to the doctor's and to classes. It's been such a blessing. I don't know what I would have done if I hadn't gotten this place. I was desperate, and I did think about doing drugs back then because I was so scared. This place has given me my independence, which is the whole purpose of the program. Something had to change, and this program helped me make the change. I have become an independent adult here. That's really something that I'm proud of."

The Workshop

Across the gravel parking lot where Crisis Center volunteers and clients (those few who have cars) park each weekday, hunches a squat, sprawling, one-story red brick building that still looks like the warehouse it once was. This is the Joseph House Workshop, the last of the ministries that Sr.Mary Elizabeth envisioned before so many illnesses took her life—but never her visionary powers--away. The outside looks worn, almost derelict, hunkering inconspicuously amid the industrial detritus of Boundary Street. But inside, this hulking edifice hums with vitality and purpose. It is home for eight formerly homeless, jobless, and often hopeless men who have been selected from many applicants to live, work, and pray together for up to two years and to move, as the Workshop handbook states, "from homelessness to permanent stable living, to find and maintain employment, and to reach their full potential."

Joseph House Workshop is, then, the male complement to the Village of Hope. In its aspirations is Sr. Mary Elizabeth's desire to assist these men to become self-sufficient members of society, to be moral agents who can care for their families and contribute to the public good by serving as models for other men who have somehow lost their way. Sr. Mary Elizabeth was firm in her conviction that few men had ever lost employment because they were unable to do the work. For her it was mainly a lack of personal or life skills that she was certain could be learned given sufficient time and commitment. She would see a man in the throes of a disorderly life and believe that God was calling him to a life of harmony and purpose, and that what he needed was help responding to the call.

"This is our classroom. Lots of work gets done in here, lots of work." Rudy Drummond, the Resident Assistant Program Director, is obviously proud of Joseph House Workshop and what it has achieved. He's a big bear of a man, with gentle eyes and a ready laugh and he has an insider's knowledge of the program. "I'm a graduate," he confesses, laughing. He surveys the classroom, which is just big enough to contain a long conference table and ten chairs, a file cabinet and, mounted on one wall, a white board, and on another, a bulletin board to which are pinned program suggestions and schedules.

"The men spend the first three months of their residency going to class every day except Sunday." Rudy picks up a book lying on the cabinet. "This is the heart and soul of the education here," he says, holding up Rick Warren's The Purpose-Driven Life.

"This, and Joyce Meyers' <u>Battlefield of the Mind</u>. Dr. Art Marsh leads the discussions. He's an addiction specialist and does relapse prevention. Most of the guys in here are addicts." Art is the Program Director. He and Rudy both are recovering addicts. "So, there's mandatory class every day for the first three months. And everyone must attend a 12-step meeting every day, including Sunday."

"We also have mandatory prayers each morning in here"—and Rudy gestures toward a large airy room furnished with comfortable sofas, coffee tables, easy chairs and a television. "Part of prayer time is devoted to reading passages from the Bible and asking the men to offer their insights. You'll notice that we run a pretty tight schedule here, but within the confines of it we encourage the residents to offer suggestions to improve the program, and to rely more and more on their own insights to class texts and the Bible readings. We want to foster a spirit of mature independence."

Beyond the classroom and living room, the Workshop features a computer room (with six monitors the men use for school work and for employment searches), a large bright dining room, a spacious kitchen, a huge pantry, an industrial-sized freezer and refrigerator, two large washers and two dryers, two small bedrooms for the night monitors, and a residential dormitory. The walls are decorated with illustrated plaques inscribed, "Be thankful," and "Trust in the Lord," and one compelling, moving print depicts a young man, seen from the back, being embraced so lovingly and so tenderly by Jesus.

"You can't help noticing how clean and neat it all is," Rudy says, obviously pleased. "The guys are responsible for it all, for the class and living room and entrance area, the halls and the bathrooms. And they take turns cooking, and serving, and cleaning up after each meal. And meals are mandatory, too. Sr. Mary Elizabeth was very big on community. She wanted the men here to know what strength there can be in belonging to a supportive and trusting fellowship."

Rudy's job at the Workshop fills him with joy, he declares. He's finishing a two-year degree in Human Services and intends to get an undergraduate degree in Drug and Alcohol Counseling. He started doing crack and cocaine when he was sixteen years old. He's thirty-six now. When he was twenty-seven he entered an eighteen month rehab program. He got a good job, working for ASDI, a subsidiary of Pfizer. "I was sober for 4 ½ years, gave up drugs, cigarettes, cursing." Then he got cocky and decided he could handle his addiction on his own and within 6 months he was "back out there" in the drug culture again. "I lost everything. I spent all my energies searching for the next high. Needless to say, I lost my job—I just walked away from it, actually. The only thing that could stop me from using were the cops."

One day not long after he began using again, he confessed to a friend that he was in deep trouble. His friend had him admitted to Kirkwood Detox in Wilmington. From there he went through a string of rehab programs. "The last was called Serenity

Place. After months in treatment, I was confident I could stay clean. I tried to do it without help, without God. I sort of white-knuckled it for 2 ½ years. I left the Bible behind. I was miserable. The bottom for me was seeing the look on my mother's face when I arrived home during this stretch. I didn't have any place to stay. I had no money, no friends, no support. So I went home, hauling all my worldly possessions in two large trash bags." Rudy begins to cry as he relates this awful encounter. "My mother told me a long time later that she couldn't speak to me, she was so devastated. 'All I could think about was that this was my son, and he lives out of trash bags.' "

Rudy was so humiliated and so sorry for the heartache he was causing his family. They had no faith or trust in their son. They had already been heartbroken from his previous relapses. His father had been volunteering at the Crisis Center for several years and knew about the Workshop. He told Rudy he could get in there if he would go to meetings and provide proof of living drug-free for six months.

In the Workshop he began to listen less to his emotions and tried to direct his life in accordance with principles he found in the Bible. "I gave God permission to run the show. Drugs and alcohol were the greatest source of my defeat but now they have become the greatest source of my strength. My whole purpose now is to let God help me fight this thing and to help as many people out of the fire as I can. I am so grateful to be where I am, doing what I'm doing."

He says that today he is offering his life as a moral support and guide for the men in the program. Rudy never met Sr. Mary Elizabeth, but he is certain his life of responsible sobriety and service is a testimony to her vision.

The Last Years

Mother Goose

Sr. Mary Elizabeth humbly accepted the affection and endured the adulation of more and more people in Salisbury, in Maryland, and throughout the nation. As word of her ministry spread, so too did the recognition that conferred with it the rewards and burdens of such notoriety. It was not long after being honored with the Lumen Christi Award from the Extension Society in Chicago in 1989 that it became common for newspaper and magazine articles to refer to Sr. Mary Elizabeth as "the Mother Teresa of Salisbury." For Sister, it was cause for some unease, but for others in the order it was an opportunity for them to tease Sister about her fame. Others may think of you as Mother Teresa, they proclaimed, but they knew better; to these women who lived with her and loved her, she had become "Mother Goose."

It was not that Sister reminded them of the fictional author of children's stories and poems. Their nickname for her derived from another book altogether: <u>The Medicine Wheel: Earth Astrology</u>, a collection of Native American spirit-lore that some-one had left at the convent and that quickly became a source of entertainment on winter nights at the dinner table. The book invites readers to discover their own personal totems; the Little Sisters instead made their discoveries a playful group project, and they were delighted at how many attributes Sr. Mary Elizabeth shared with the People of the Snow goose. They are, like the geese they resemble, very gregarious, thriving on company and companion-ship. They have great respect for tradition "and a real sense of obeying authority. While their minds might be breaking new frontiers, their conduct will always be very proper, bound in tradition and respectful of any authorities over them." People of the Snow goose "have minds that are able to soar and cover vast distances" even as they remain confined or at rest. They are somewhat controlling, craving order and completion.

"Sister possessed all of these qualities," said Sr. Marilyn. Long before the sisters found her de-scribed in the book, she believed she had a special affinity with the stark white geese strung out in wavy threads against the sky above the Eastern Shore. She loved hearing the geese flying over the Novitiate in the Fall, winging south ahead of the coming storms. She thought it was wonderful that they knew when it was time to go. She seemed to think of them as kindred spirits. "And they were there for her funeral on All Saints Day," Sr. Marilyn said. "They flew over St Francis de Sales Church as the pall bearers were putting Sister's coffin in the hearse, lots of them in one of those 'V' formations, and there was a flock of them feeding near the lake in Parsons Cemetery during the burial service. She always felt a strong attraction to those birds, especially after we showed her how much like them she was! If you visit her grave in Parsons, you'll see a flying goose carved above her name. Her name's misspelled, but the flying goose accurately captures her spirit!"

Dialogue With My Body

In her 80's, Sr. Mary Elizabeth struggled with health problems that had begun years before and were aggravated by her ceaseless labor for Joseph House and for the Little Sisters. She refused to give over control of the order or the several ministries to others despite being told often, especially by Monsignor McGlynn, that all her works would not survive beyond her life if she didn't pass those responsibilities to others. She had been diagnosed with Chronic Obstructive Pulmonary Disease which became more pronounced as the years passed. In a reflection she wrote while on retreat at the Jesuit Center for Spiritual Growth in Wernersville Pennsylvania in 1982 (22 years before her death), which she titled "A Dialogue With My Body," she acknowledged how the simple act of breathing had become a struggle.

Here in her dialogue, she focuses on her chest: "My chest has served me well for many years. In the past 10 years, however, it has continued to cause me trouble.... I used to pride myself on how long I could hold my breath underwater while swimming. And I loved to think of Jesus in the Eucharist coming to rest in the strong house of my chest.

> Chest - We seem to be at odds so often these days.
>
> Me - You are not what you used to be.
>
> Chest - I am worn; I do my best.
>
> Me - I fear you may be in for worse days.
>
> Chest - I try to give you enough oxygen and to serve you well. But you do not do much to help me.
>
> Me - I sometimes wish that God would relieve you. I am tired, and embarrassed, and handicapped by your chronic cough....
>
> Chest- You have to expect some things at your age.
>
> Me - I just want you to keep well enough to let me finish the things I've started.
>
> Chest - Then follow the practices that will keep me well.
>
> Me - I do!
>
> Chest - But too late.

Me - With God's help it is never too late,
and I do wish God would help – after all
He actually comes to rest in you every
day."

Her playful little dialogue indicates that she was
already aware of her breathing problems before
she was 70 years old, and as she aged, she coughed
more, had more trouble breathing.

As she aged, the symptoms of the Chronic
Obstructive Pulmonary Disease became more
discernible. She coughed more, had more trouble
breathing. Then in 1992, she suffered a severe heart
attack while flying to Texas to visit with former volunteers who had been with her in Baltimore. " She
was very stubborn, wanted to go alone," Sr. Connie
said. "But we all got together and refused to let
her, so Sr. Marilyn went with her, thank God."   Sr.
Marilyn recalls Sr. Mary Elizabeth being enthralled
by the vibrant pink hues of the early sky above the
dark clouds beneath the plane's flight. Sr. Mary Elizabeth noted that they could well be flying over rain
clouds showering the earth below, yet their sky was
shining with the sun's light. She reflected on the
beauty of this as an image of God's ever-presence
despite the darkness and storms of our lives below.

Shortly into their flight, Sr. Mary Elizabeth had
a prolonged coughing attack. Water and an inhaler
helped to restore her breathing again, but suddenly
Sister gasped, "Is this plane spinning around?" She

sat upright, her eyes fixed, her body rigid, her right hand clenched in a fist. Spasms and pain coursed through her frail little body. Sr. Marilyn called out for help and was immediately aided by a doctor aboard the flight. He quickly assessed her condition and administered the nitroglycerine which Sister had with her in her medical case.

She experienced a crushing sensation in her chest and began to struggle for air. She spoke of the searing pain in her chest and the spasms in her body. Despite the excruciating pain, Sister stayed conscious throughout her struggle. Nitroglycerin provided some help, but because of the urgency and gravity of her condition—the pain now radiated to her back and shoulders—the doctor told the plane's crew that they would have to make an emergency landing as soon as possible. Roanoke, Virginia was the nearest airport, 15 minutes away.

Sr. Marilyn prayed and was joined in prayer by several passengers who wanted to reassure Sr. Mary Elizabeth (and themselves) that all would be well. As Sr. Marilyn put it, "we all had to abide by faith and abandonment, two guides by which Sister always lived, and trust that God would hold her in His light as we struggled in our darkness of unknowing and powerlessness."

The crisis touched many lives. The physician assisting Sr. Mary Elizabeth wept; he and his wife were on their way to bury her father. The past two days had been very difficult for him, and Sister's grave situation heightened his feeling of powerlessness. "I tried to console him," Sr. Marilyn said, "telling him that I was so very sorry for his loss, and yet so grateful for his being there. Perhaps, somehow, out of his father-in-law's death would come restored health for Sr. Mary Elizabeth. Somehow, I said, God is present and watching over us in all of these hours. I'm sure now that that was true."

The staff at Roanoke Memorial Hospital concluded that Sr. Mary Elizabeth had suffered a massive heart attack. Neurological tests pointed to two strokes in the brain caused by two blood clots. Sister began having seizures while she was in CCU, and Sr. Marilyn was counseled to face the likelihood of Sister's death or permanent impairment if she pulled through.

Srs. Connie and Patricia arrived later that day; Tom and Vicki Anselmi, the Texas friends they had been on their way to visit, arrived that day, too. Fathers Dan McGlynn and John Abrahams arrived later that night, and, by Saturday, all of the Little Sisters were in Roanoke. "We thought she was going to die," Sr. Connie recalled. "We were so fortunate—Fr. Abrahams paid for our fares, and the bishop in Roanoke let us stay in Madonna House which was affiliated with Catherine Doherty, a spiritual teacher whom Sister admired and whose life, like Sister's, was full of the love of God." But the sisters wanted to be with Sr. Mary Elizabeth, and so they spent most of their time in the hospital, crowded around her bed, praying, singing, trying to get her to respond to them in some way, to give them a sign that she was going to be alright. And suddenly, during a prayer, she awoke, and spoke to them, asking what had happened, and they knew they had witnessed a miracle—the recovery was so dramatic, so quick. Sr. Mary Elizabeth, they believed, had been called back to serve, a call first heard some 70 years ago.

As she recovered her health, she recovered also that urgent need to be back at work with the poor. During the days of recovery that followed, Sr. Mary Elizabeth once again exhibited that vibrant sense of humor that her friends had feared they would never witness again. As Sister began her own journey back to health, she was inspired with an even greater resolve to become like those who reach out from their own powerlessness to heal and comfort others, to become that Christ Incarnate, helping others in their journey to healing.

Sr. Mary Elizabeth eventually returned to Salisbury, arriving at the convent in an ambulance where she was greeted, as she lay on a stretcher, by three deliriously happy dogs—and by the city fathers of Salisbury gathered in the convent chapel to present her with a Rotary award. Clearly there would be little time to rest and restore her depleted strength! Now she faced weeks of therapy and medication, but for her the important journey had begun again. The prognosis was good for complete recovery, a clear sign to her that the Lord was calling her to continue in her ministry.

But her breathing problems persisted. Dr. Joe Badros, her primary physician, loved Sister deeply and wanted her to work less and conserve her energy. For what? she'd ask, if not to have more strength to do more work. She would frustrate him, and he would badger her: You must get these tests! No, I will not! Then I won't be your doctor! Oh yes you will! Dr. Badros told her if she didn't sleep with the dogs in her room, she'd suffer less from her cough. She denied vehemently sleeping with the dogs, failing to confess that they slept on the floor under her desk in her bedroom. Then she suffered a series of falls that were a consequence of her increasing frailty. One day while making tea she slipped on one of the dog's tennis balls in the kitchen and broke her pelvis. On an earlier occasion she was walking one of the dogs in the neighborhood of the convent when it took off after another dog. Sister had wrapped the leash around her wrist, "and suddenly," she reported, "I was looking at blades of grass." That time, she had broken her wrist.

Then, on July 4th, 2000, she had a major fall. She caught her foot on a step in the novitiate kitchen and fell, hitting her head on the counter and on the floor. She fractured her arm in four places, and cut a gash across her eye. Then she fell in the living room of the Novitiate while eating her dinner and watching the news. Her eyes were so blackened by that fall, Sr. Connie said, "she looked like a little raccoon." That required another ambulance trip and hospitalization in Salisbury.

In October, 2004, she went to the hospital with pneumonia. Her cough weakened her; she had trouble breathing. She got antibiotics from another doctor because Dr. Badros was out of town, and returned to Princess Anne with the medicines. When Dr. Badros came back and saw her, he told her she had to go to the hospital. She refused. Dr. Badros told her if she wasn't better from the medications by the weekend (three days), she had to come up to Salisbury and go into the hospital. She said okay, but didn't really mean it. Before she went back to Princess Anne, she agreed to go to the hospital and get a chest X-ray. While she waited at the hospital clinic, she told Sr. Marilyn that she'd be much better if instead of getting an X-ray she could get an Arby's milkshake. A mocha shake, she said, smiling with childlike delight.

She didn't get better. She died in Peninsula General Medical Center in Salisbury in the early morning of October 27th. Sr. Mary Joseph stayed with the body until hospital orderlies took her to the morgue. The people from Zeller Funeral Home got the body from there. The first person the funeral director called was Dave Pogge. Dave was another close friend of Sr. Mary Elizabeth's and a great financial supporter of Sister's various missions. As President and Chief Operating Officer of Mountaire Corp. and Mountaire Farms, he directed one of the largest privately held businesses in the U.S., but he always had time to advise Sr. Mary Elizabeth and be advised by her in his turn.

He confided to her one day early in 2004 that one of his favorite leisure activities was woodworking. She might have had a premonition that her time on earth was soon coming to an end. She said to him, "Good! You can make my coffin!" He was shocked by her request, took it as a jest, then realized she was serious, and finally agreed, telling her it would be an honor for him. "But," she said, "nothing fancy. Make it simple, just a simple pine box." He finished it a few months before she died, and the photo of the two of them standing in front of the coffin, their faces radiating delight, shows that Sr. Mary Elizabeth was pleased with the finished product.

Zeller's took possession of the coffin from a grieving Mr. Pogge and on October 31st, All Souls Day, Sr. Mary Elizabeth's earthly remains were brought to St. Francis de Sales Church. The Little Sisters of Jesus and Mary were there to escort the casket through the throngs of mourners already gathered to say goodbye to this nun who had done so much to comfort the poor of their community. For several hours following noon Mass on that Sunday, the line moved slowly past the open casket before the altar. The viewing was stopped at 9pm and the casket was moved to the Chapel of Saints off the vestibule of the church. The Little Sisters kept vigil through the night, and when the church was opened again early on November 1st, throngs more of her grieving friends crowded into the vestibule for one last visitation with this little woman they loved and mourned. Finally, the casket was closed, and moved to the front of the church for the funeral Mass.

"It was a perfect Autumn day," Sr. Marilyn re-called. "Gorgeous skies and radiant, fresh air. We followed the casket out into the day, and there were police mounted on horses, dressed in their finery, red jackets with gold buttons and high black boots. It was very stately, very regal, very fitting—a funeral fit for a queen." The mounted honor guard escorted the procession of hundreds of cars to Parson's Cemetery. And above them, as if guiding her on her way, a huge 'V' of geese accompanied the vast cortege.

Today, if you visit the grave, you notice that the marker is on the edge of a large empty plot. "We bought plots for 23. We were thinking big," laughs Sr. Connie. Now the plot contains only Sr. Mary Elizabeth and Sr. Catherine Hayes, who died in 1992 and whose little stone has almost been completely obscured by the weather of 22 years. You will also notice the engraved goose flying perpetually above the nun who was embarrassed by the comparison with Mother Teresa but who loved being the Mother Goose for her little order. And if you visit, don't be surprised if you see a flock of these huge birds waddling silently, almost protectively, nearby.

In Her Own Words

From an interview with Dan McDonald

The Little Sisters of the Poor impressed me so much with their total dedication to their work and their total detachment from material things. They sought to help those people who had nothing, and they were resolved to provide those poor with comforts otherwise unavailable to them. But the sisters themselves did not seek out those comforts for themselves. That attitude of complete lack of attachment to material things deeply attracted me to them.

I must confess that when I joined the Little Sisters of the Poor, I didn't much care for old people at all. I certainly didn't want to make them my life's work! I had to learn to cherish them, and I did, and I missed them terribly when I left the order. And even now I just yearn to go out and find elderly in need and try to make their days easier for them, try to give them whatever they need to make life less burdensome. I sometimes wish I were ten people. Then I could do that.

It's terrible to be old and alone; oh my God, it's

just terrible. Now I know that more than ever—how terrible it is to be old and sick, confused and alone. I am convinced that many, many old people suffer unnecessarily because they misuse their medicine, and I know that we could easily solve that problem in most instances. So I am hoping, before I die, that God will send me someone who wants to create a program for this purpose and we can add this to the work we are doing.

There's much to be done that we haven't even begun to do. We need to create a cadre of volunteers to visit the aged, to take away the fear so many of them have that there's no one to watch out for them. It's that frightening insecurity that is so insupportable and that makes them so miserable. We also need a coordinated program to make our sisters and volunteers more aware of the fears and horrors that assail many of the children in the families we help. Such fear can disfigure these children for the rest of their lives, makes them into people who are afraid of everything–afraid of the future, of other people, afraid that no one will ever be decent to them because no one has ever treated them decently, kindly and with respect. We need to find a way to expose those fears and help the children vanquish them. Not to educate them, to ensure they will be successful, but to help them to have peace of heart and mind, and to know God and know that He loves them, and that there is a way—prayer—to communicate with Him and to be aware of His loving presence.

I hate seeing people in fear. I hate seeing animals in fear. I know I've become attached to my dogs because they were abused and neglected. I didn't especially want to own pets. I just wanted to make sure that animals that had been mistreated knew they were loved and cared for so they can experience security and peace of heart. But, you know, these things, the suffering of others and other creatures, have been the impetus for everything I've ever done, ever since I was a child. It's just that in my own old age I've become more sensitive to how fear and insecurity impoverish a life.

Poverty doesn't bother me so much, but I have a horror of injustice. Electricity and gas to heat a home costs the same for a family living on $50 a week as it costs for a man making $3 million dollars a year. That's unjust. Gas and electric companies should install meters that take quarters so families can have gas for a bath or a meal or as much heat as they can afford. They shouldn't have all service cut off and have to pay an outrageous penalty to have it turned on again because they can't afford a monthly fee. That's unjust.

It's a wonderful way to spend your life, I'll tell you that. Truthfully, I don't expect a reward for what I've done. The work of taking care of people has been reward enough. I don't feel as if I've lived a virtuous life; honestly, I've only done what I've always wanted to do. It has been such a fulfilling life for me, a great joy overall.

There are so many injustices that bother me to death. It turns me into a warrior! I become angry, and I know I would defend anyone with my life to get an injustice righted. It doesn't bother me when people are poor because poverty, although it causes difficulty and disturbance, isn't wrong, isn't sinful. It challenges us to alleviate it. For those with faith, poverty is often a spiritual good. For those without faith, it is no more or less than an intolerable social evil. It's the same with illness. Illness can be a means to grace, or it can be the cause of self-pitying rage. It can lead to sanctification or to sin. But injustice that causes poverty—that is always sinful, always evil.

In our work we come into contact with what I tell the sisters and volunteers is slobberty, not poverty, and one of our most challenging tasks is to differentiate the two. Occasionally we will go into a house in which the family lives surrounded by rubbish, debris, the clutter of people who have never learned to care for themselves. Poverty not only breeds hopelessness; it also robs people of the most fundamental instinct for self-respect and rudimentary disciplines of cleanliness and order. They've been raised in environments of disorder and carelessness and they have absorbed those inclinations. They become part of their character and are as hard to root out as the behaviors that often intensify and prolong the poverty. So we often have two challenges, and we must be able to distinguish them. We can teach those we reach out to that they can do simple things to acquire and maintain cleanliness and order and work to instill in them an ambition for them.

I came from a home in which no matter how poor we were we never knew it because our mother kept our home so neat and clean. Occasionally there was no money for food, so my mother would take old bread and make bread soup, so we learned that there were inconveniences in life, but they couldn't defeat you or make you think less of yourself so that you ceased taking care of yourself and your surroundings. But so many poor children today are raised by parents who neglect their children, and those children grow up neglecting their children. It's terrible. But if you can enter into that world somehow and break that cycle, it's worth everything, because the good habits will spread into the community from one family to others.

If you can make one rich person comprehend the injustice of economic inequality, you will have accomplished a great deal. I mentored a young Canadian nurse while in the Little Sisters of the Poor. She was very unhappy there; she wanted to do missionary work in Latin America. I advised her to join the Dominicans, and they sent her down there to teach wealthy girls at a private college. She wrote to me, "Is this what I came down here for? Is this how I am to serve God, teaching these privileged young women?" I wrote back: "Stop complaining. God has brains; He knows what He's doing. He knows that if you teach these young women to love justice you will have helped all the poor. You want to work with the poor because it makes you feel fulfilled. Believe me, you can do more for the poor if you instill in those girls a respect for the poor and a love for justice. You'll care for hundreds of poor people that way."

My path has been slightly different from the one I put her on. I need to be among the poor. I think I got that impulse from my father. My mother was a timid and often frightened little woman. If a tramp came to the door and my father wasn't home she wouldn't open the door. She would fix them something to eat, but she'd never go out on the porch with them—she'd hand the food through the door and close it quickly. She actually seemed terrified of people who weren't exactly like her. I was the opposite. I had my father's attitude, mostly. I felt the best way to serve someone was to be out in their world with them, to show kindred with their suffering.

Reflections on Justice
[from an interview with Dan McDonald]

I believe strongly that people who work with and for the poor should share their poverty. To work for the poor, to join them in the struggle for justice, and yet to benefit in your own life from the injustice that oppresses them—that's not a very good example. We should not be comfortably employed by companies that treat some of their workers unfairly. I have always been more devoted to justice than I have been to the elimination of poverty. I'm not afraid of poverty. I understand that it can be deadly, I understand that it can result in the impoverishment of children's minds if there's insufficient funds to educate them, or if they grow up with parents who are so demoralized by poverty that they can't care about them, don't know enough to care about them. These are severe handicaps, but they're not nearly as crippling as injustice is. Of course it is often the case that the poverty is a direct consequence of injustice. But poverty is not the only consequence of injustice. I have witnessed affluent children damaged by parents too negligent, too heedless, to give their children the guidance and love they need. These children don't suffer from physical hunger, but you can see in their faces that they are spiritually and emotionally emaciated.

What we need is justice for all children. And it is the same even for animals!

God, we know, is just, and we are created in his image, and therefore have an obligation to imitate Him in every way. Our Holy Father has insisted that we can't have peace without justice. Martin Luther King and his followers who struggled for racial equality echoed that assertion in one of their most forceful rallying cries. Injustice is the cause of every war, and war causes more human suffering than disease, natural disasters, poverty. No justice, no peace. No justice, nothing but turmoil, pain, misery. For children! Imagine it! Yet we allow it to continue, and in some cultures to prevail.

There can be no justice wherever there is greed. Justice, then, is as much an antidote to greed as to violence and brutality. It is, in fact, a corrective to all the conspicuous vices. The fight against injustice begets virtue. Saint Joseph is my model for the just man. His devotion to his family, his quiet indifference to his own desires, his humble labor and submission to the will of God—these to me are the hallmarks of the just man, the man of charity, self-sacrifice, patience, magnanimity. He is surely one of our models in the house named for him!

If everybody were just, everybody would have what they need to live. I am convinced that all we need is that one virtue. If you strive for justice, you'll have the others. That is why I have always maintained that poverty is not a great difficulty in life if you have justice. In a just world everyone blessed with abundance would share it with those who don't have enough to survive. In a just world there would be no poverty.

The social service aspect of Joseph House is an attempt to restore justice. We need to train our volunteers not so much to alleviate the poverty with a check, but to examine why people we're trying to help can't remedy the problems for themselves. What injustice, if any, prevents them from helping themselves? Everyone has the right—and the responsibility--to help themselves. What accounts for their lack of self-reliance? Lack of education? Then we need to provide means by which they can get an education. This is only just. Are they victims of unscrupulous landlords or employers or public servants? This, too, is injustice, and we need to do whatever we can to correct the condition. The solution is rarely in the stopgap check that relieves the suffering momentarily but not the long-term causes of the suffering.

It often seems as if there is a continual war between the weak and the strong. Who can countenance such an inequitable state of affairs? The victory of the mean and the strong over the weak! I have to resist turning away from such total injustice because it is so offensive. I have to keep seeking ways of ending the war, of bringing justice, and therefore peace.

And our nation's wars do little beyond making everybody poorer; our money is spent killing other people and destroying other countries. Are we war criminals? Are we aggressors whose actions are as brutalizing as those whose greed and indifference causes suffering among the poor? These questions consume my days. Are we instruments of God or the Devil? Can wars that kill so many on both sides, that destroy innocent lives, that waste money that could be spent alleviating the suffering of the poor, spent on health care and education—can such acts be good? Can they be sanctioned by God? I don't understand it. It's like a kind of insanity. And children, who are most often the victims of these things, are blameless. The babies, the infants, even the fetuses. Doctors will perform miraculous operations on fetuses to repair physical defects, yet they countenance the abortion of these same life forms. This is surely the slaughter of the innocents in our time. Incredible. A satanic insanity that has infected America and the world.

The only way to tackle these injustices is to pray to God. He is the only one who knows how this butchery can be vanquished. I for one cannot find the compelling argument to convince even a sane person that abortion is murder, that war is murder, that greed is murder.

Dorothy Day found the words. She spoke out lucidly and fearlessly against everything that was unjust. She was willing to go to jail for justice, to march and preach and obstruct for justice. Others have chosen to stay behind, tending the fires at the camp site, as it were, feeding the hungry, comforting the afflicted. These are humbler tasks, but they are essential, the works ordained to Martha.

From an interview with WSEM-FM's Bob Franklin,
January, 1992

Homelessness is a very complex problem. It seems the more we do to try to help the homeless, the more the government does to make life more difficult for them. The government has not only turned its back on the poor; it seems to be working against them. It has set up barriers that make it more difficult for organizations, businesses, other institutions to help the poor. Businesses today seem more interested in profit than in corporate good works. Their greed means that there's less money for the middle class, which means there's less they have to give to the really poor people in this country, to the destitute and homeless. The worse things get, the more economizing the average family does. I don't know where it's going to end. It seems to me that what we should be doing is creating jobs, therefore helping people help themselves.

It's harmful to tell people, well, you can't be dependent on society anymore, without giving them a way to be independent. There is no justice in this kind of treatment, and without justice we have nothing. Until business and government invest in justice, there won't be enough work for people to do to support themselves and their families, which is what most people want in life. We can't say to people, we're not going to give you any more food, but we don't expect you to starve as a result. This is illogical, and it's what the government is doing. I'm always happy to hear about companies that furlough everyone rather than laying workers off. And landlords can do their part by not raising rent during times of economic stagnation and by being aware of their tenants' changing circumstances. Everyone has to cooperate or we can't make it through hard times such as this.

I don't want you to think that I am in favor of welfare as a long-term solution for a family's woes. I'm not. I know very well how crippling, how downright disabling the welfare system can be. I am in favor of partnerships of businesses and the government and volunteers that do everything they can to create jobs for welfare clients. When welfare becomes a way of life, the soul goes out of a man or a woman. They lose all hope. Families fall apart. Fathers abandon their children. And these children, left with no one to teach them how to care for themselves and others, are in turn incapacitated by the debilitating scheme that was meant to assist them. Generation follows generation. What can we do to strengthen the family? That should be our goal. Without family, people have nothing. That's what I work for always—to help people become family strong.

For clients seeking help from Joseph House, we try to instill in them one central conviction, and that is that they are their own best source of help. We can pay someone's rent this week so that he's not thrown out on the street, but who will pay it next week? This help I give you today is really no help if it doesn't restore in you some hope and a sense of purpose. Our main effort is to help clients see how they can become independent, how they can help themselves. Sometimes all it takes is a little encouragement from another, someone saying to you, I'm here to support you in your struggle to pull yourself up. We understand the sad passivity of many people in need, how they feel helpless. We're successful if we can lift that burden from them, help them find their strength, help them feel God's love for them, let them know they're not alone. Of course, our other job is to make sure that those who have much are introduced to the have-nothings in their midst!

So, we soldier on, trusting in God's love for us and for everyone. I know that life was not easy for Him when He came to Earth, but that didn't keep Him from His ministry of saving us. I believe that if you have faith in God, He will give you the means to do His work. One of AA's main tenants describes how we live in Joseph House. We take one day at a time, each day as it comes. I get up in the morning and face whatever faces me that day. Then I go to bed, after thanking God for all His blessings, and I sleep, and I get up the next day to discover what I will face next. I've been doing that for almost sixty years now, so I guess I can do it for a few more. I have so much to be grateful for. I've seen volunteers become passionate advocates for the poor, and that lifts me up. And when someone who has been beaten down by poverty and injustice rises up, breaks the chains of penury and becomes independent—well, that is a tremendous joy.

Words of Farewell to the Baltimore Ministry,
September 1, 1974

The Joseph House since its beginning in October of 1965 has been an organization that identified with the poor and the oppressed. Our purpose was "To become like the poor in all things, to understand and to enter into their existence." During these past nine years we have had many dedicated lay people and religious who have carried out this philosophy to whatever depth each one understood and felt capable. Thousands of individuals and families have been served from Joseph House and surely to a few of these families and individuals it has made a difference in a somewhat permanent manner.

We have been able to carry out this work because of three factors: God's grace, faithful and generous benefactors and board members, and faithful and generous staff.

We hope none of this will change in spite of the fact that there are some major changes taking place in other ways. It has become evident to most of us working with the poor that for the most part the percentage of change that has come about in the lives of the poor receiving material help from us has been rather low. In cases of true oppression such as the elderly who do not receive sufficient income for today's high costs and who are really desperate, we want to continue to be materially available. For the unforeseen crisis such as illness, robbery, fire, and so forth, we want to be materially available. But for the great mass of welfare recipients from whom our society has robbed all motivation we want to become a witness and a source of motivation. In order to establish this type of witness we must of necessity build a deep foundation of love within ourselves which recognizes that often empowerment and independence and dignity are the greatest gifts we can give to others.

In "Pedagogy of the Oppressed," Paulo Freire writes, "No matter where the oppressed are found the act of love is commitment to their cause — the cause of liberation. And this commitment, because it is loving, is dialogical." How can there be a dialogue if there is no encounter, if there is only silent and momentary relief that fosters dependency?

Again, Freire: "At the point of encounter there are neither utter ignoramuses nor perfect sages; there are only men who are attempting, together, to learn more than they now know. . . .Founding itself upon love, humility and faith, dialogue becomes a horizontal relationship; of which mutual trust between the participants is the logical consequence. It would be a contradiction in terms if dialogue — loving, humble and full of faith — did not produce this climate of mutual trust, which leads the collaborators into very close partnership of equality."

This desire to bridge the gap between the poor, the oppressed and ourselves and to thereby help to bring about dialogue and true understanding leads us into a new way of life. And without entering at this moment into the depth of how we hope to bring this about, we would simply like to say that our ultimate goal is to share with the disadvantaged and oppressed a mutual understanding of God, His life and concern for all of us, His presence among us especially in the person of Jesus, the fact that salvation is available to all, and the practice and power of prayer.

In order to accomplish so great a task we feel that our own spirituality must be considerably deepened. So Sr. Patricia and I are studying the spirituality of Fr. Charles de Foucauld known to his followers as Brother Charles of Jesus. Born in 1858 in Strasbourg and killed in 1916 in Africa, he was "part soldier, part intelligence agent, part monk and part hermit" and founder of a religious congregation devoted to work and contemplation. He is the spiritual father of the Little Brothers and Little Sisters of Jesus and the Little Brothers and Little Sisters of the Gospel.

We hope to spend this year laying our foundation, spelling out the differences that warrant our separate existence and being good neighbors to the poor around us, working at the store, keeping the school going, writing our rule and beginning to live a contemplative life. We trust you will continue to help us with your prayers and support, and whatever available time you can give us. You are always welcome to come by to see us — to see how things are progressing and avail yourselves of our hospitality. We will open the house to works of evangelization such as conferences, prayer groups, and retreats for those unable to afford them elsewhere. We hope that this will help bring about an atmosphere in which the poor can learn their own real worth, and from that realization begin to be motivated to change their own lives — to rid their lives of the sources of unhappiness and discontent.

And so, Farewell! Since its beginning, Joseph House has had more than its share of goodbyes and farewells, but the thank you and goodbye that we must say this time are really deep ones. So many of you have been the "soul" of Joseph House for hundreds of people. Your service has been marked by self sacrificing love and a genuineness that proclaims sincerity from start to finish. There are hundreds of people who will never forget your easy going zeal and total understanding. Your service to God and the people has never been marked by half heartedness or self-seeking.

Feed My Lambs!: Just as before people come to our door daily asking for food. We want to continue to feed their bodies but to feed their spirits, too, so that they can and will join in the Body of Christ as missionaries of His work. Feed my lambs! This is our command, our burden, and our perfection.